THE PAS...
OF EAST ANGLIA

THE TALES HISTORY FORGOT

ABIGAIL PULLEN-GAME

Best wishes
(signature)

Self-Published by Abigail Pullen-Game

First published in Great Britain in 2022

ISBN 978-1-3999-2201-2

Printed and bound in Great Britain by TJ Books
Designed by Softwood Self-Publishing

CONTENTS

CHAPTER ONE - Tudor Tales   Page

CHAPTER TWO - Influential Women

CHAPTER THREE - Soldiers' Stories

CHAPTER FOUR - Famous Faces

CHAPTER FIVE - East Anglian Tales

CHAPTER SIX - Suffolk Specials

CHAPTER ONE

TUDOR TALES

1. ELIZABETH TILNEY

It's Thursday, 28th November 1489

A woman stands in full view of Elizabeth of York as she enjoys her meal of spiced wines and sweet cakes. Elizabeth dabs her lips whilst the dishes are removed and begins to pray for the safe delivery of a healthy prince.

Prayers delivered, the noblemen leave the room and twenty ladies lead her to a magnificently carved oak bed. Covering it is a heavy duvet embroidered with neat red roses, the emblem of the House of Lancaster. Above, a gold canopy casts a shadow over the prone queen who is breathing through yet another contraction. By 9.00 p.m. the child is born. A princess, she is to be named Margaret Tudor.

Two days have passed and the women enter the light and airy, yet elegant porch of St Margaret's church, Westminster, London. The lavishly dressed entourage (in their silks and neatly stitched golden-threaded attire) stand forth and promise to protect the little princess. The woman takes her place and makes her promises before God. She now takes on the role of Godmother to a royal dynasty which will fascinate people for hundreds of years to come.

Elizabeth Tilney was born on 4th April 1446 at Ashwell Thorpe manor in Norfolk. Her parents were Elizabeth Cheney and Frederick Tilney, who spent most of their days in attendance of the royals as members of the court. Her grandmother was a direct descendant of the Welsh prince Gruffydd II Ap Madog.

In 1446, Elizabeth's' father Frederick died, leaving her the heiress to his vast estates. Her mother remarried in the December to Sir John Say, a speaker in the House of Commons. This union left Elizabeth with seven siblings and she lived a fairly uneventful childhood, receiving a good education and all the skills of a noble lady.

At twenty she married Sir Humphrey Bourchier from Halstead, Essex with whom she had one son and two daughters.

Elizabeth served as lady in waiting to the Queen Consort, Elizabeth Woodville, and proudly held her train at her coronation in May 1465.

In 1470 Elizabeth accompanied Elizabeth Woodville into sanctuary for the first time inside Westminster Abbey.

Edward the future king was born on a cold and frosty day in November. The second time Woodville took sanctuary, she watched her two sons being taken to the Tower of London, never to be seen again. This led to one of the most famous mysteries of the era.

Elizabeth's husband Humphrey was sadly killed on 14th April 1471, fighting on the Yorkist side at The Battle of Barnet, one of many vital battles in the ongoing Wars of the Roses. He was buried at Westminster Abbey.

On 30th April 1472 King Henry VII arranged for Elizabeth to be married to Thomas Howard, the 2nd Duke of Norfolk, from Stoke by Nayland, Suffolk. The marriage proved to be a great success, producing ten children. All flourished, but one daughter in particular, Elizabeth, married Thomas Boleyn, making Tilney the grandmother of Henry VIII's great love Anne Boleyn. She was also grandmother to Katherine Howard, (another wife of Henry VIII) and two more of her granddaughters were two of Henry's mistresses, Elizabeth Carew and Mary Boleyn, sister to Anne.

Thomas was injured at the battle of Bosworth whilst fighting for the future king Richard III (a close friend of Thomas and the Howards). The punishment for fighting for the wrong side saw Thomas imprisoned in the Tower of London for several years as well as losing his dukedom of Norfolk. Elizabeth was fortunate and held on to her lands. During her husband's imprisonment Elizabeth moved into London, close to St Katherine's by the Tower. During this time, she wrote to John Paston (a gentleman and landowner). The letter mentioned that he had previously offered her horses to transport her children back to Thorpe, Norfolk.

An agonizing three years later, Thomas was released and his titles and land were restored to him. He decided to enter the service of Henry VII who needed a good experienced fighter for his wars with the Scots.

In November 1487 the reunited couple attended the coronation of Elizabeth of York (Henry VII's wife) and Elizabeth was appointed a lady of the bedchamber. She was further honoured to be joint godmother to Princess Margaret Tudor. Richard III was crowned in July 1483 and Thomas (with Elizabeth by his side) attended the ceremony to support their friend and attend to the needs of his queen, Ann Neville.

Elizabeth passed away on 4th April 1497 without ever having earned the title of Duchess of Norfolk and was buried at the nuns' choir of the Convent of Minoresses outside Aldgate, London. In her will she left a generous contribution to the poor people of Whitechapel and Hackney. Just four months after Elizabeth's death, Thomas obtained permission from the church and married her cousin Agnes Tilney, fathering a further six children.

Elizabeth is forever remembered in a poem by John Skelton (Poet Laureate to Henry VIII) called the Garland of Laurel, recalling a time when he was a guest of Elizabeth's and she placed a garland of laurel worked in silks, gold and pearls on his head as a sign of homage. Elizabeth is also remembered on a stained-glass window at the Holy Trinity church in Long Melford, Suffolk.

2. MARY TUDOR

It's Thursday, 20th July 1533

A bustling town readies for an event like no living countryman has ever witnessed before. A lavish affair fit for a princess. Fit for a queen.

Beloved by the Suffolk people, Mary Tudor (the former Queen of France) leaves her home at Westhorpe Hall, Suffolk for her procession through the market town of Bury St Edmunds. A respectful hush spreads through the crowd as a train of a hundred men bearing torches files through the streets. A hearse pulled by six black horses enters the town on its journey to the Benedictine Abbey.

Draped in black velvet and embossed with her coat of arms, the lead-lined coffin is crowned with a single wooden effigy displaying the young regal Mary complete with golden sceptre in hand. The richly decorated canopy sits above, carried by four of the Duke of Suffolk's knights. The standard bearers surround the sad procession, followed by the richly clothed family of the deceased. Hundreds follow, ending with the chief mourner, her eldest child, leading her little family of her beloved husband Brandon's heirs.

Mary Tudor was born on 18th March 1497 to King Henry VII and his Queen Elizabeth of York at Sheen (later Richmond) Palace, London. One of four children, her father spoiled his little princess, showering her with gifts. Erasmus wrote of the three-year-old Mary that 'nature never formed anything more beautiful' and complimented her proud father on her shining golden hair. A picture-perfect family, Henry did everything to provide his offspring with the perfect childhood. However, not even a king can change the future.

Tragically in 1502 Arthur, Marys' brother and heir to the throne, died leaving the family stunned and his young wife Catherine of Aragon a widow. This sad event was quickly followed by the death of Mary's mother Elizabeth and her new-born child.

In 1509 at just thirteen Mary was orphaned when her father contracted tuberculosis and died, followed by her grandmother just two months later.

In a bold move Mary was betrothed to King Louis XII of France, a sickly man of fifty-two, and eighteen-year-old Mary agreed. However, she made a pact with Henry VIII (her surviving brother), stating that when the French king died, she could choose her own match. Three months into her new role as Queen of France her husband was dead.

Henry sent the handsome Charles Brandon to bring Mary home and, in a defiant act of treason, they married in secret, incurring the wrath of Henry who fined them heavily. A formal wedding was celebrated months later setting the love match in stone.

Mary spent many of the next eighteen years in Suffolk at her home Westhorpe Hall where she bore Brandon four children. However, her health was poor and she passed away on 25th June 1533 aged thirty-seven. She was buried after a lavish funeral at the Abbey at Bury St Edmunds, Suffolk. As was the custom of the time neither her brother nor her husband attended the service.

On the dissolution of the Abbey, Mary's remains were relocated to the nearby St Mary's church where her simple resting place remains to this day.

3. MARY BOLEYN

It's Tuesday, 4th March 1522

A celebration is under way within Cardinal Wolsey's home, York Palace. Eight beautiful ladies are dressed in white satin and wearing bejewelled caps over their thick lustrous hair. All eight ladies are positioned inside a model of a castle built at the end of the hall. The towers are illuminated, give the effect of a fire raging through the building. Each girl has a virtue embroidered upon her cloak, which represents one of the eight virtues of an ideal wife or mistress and each is being held captive by one of the eight vices, all boys from the Chapel Royal.

The girl representing the virtue of kindness was more beautiful than all the other girls put together. She was just fourteen yet well versed in the practice of courtly pastimes. In direct competition with her sister, she acted her heart out, eager to attract the attention of the powerful men watching.

However, that girl was Lady Mary who would suffer a brutal betrayal and was destined to be known as just the other Boleyn girl.

Mary Boleyn was born between 1499 and 1503, the date a subject of continued debate. Her father Thomas and mother Elizabeth née Howard were well respected and frequent visitors to the court of King Henry VIII and his queen Katherine of Aragon.

Mary was one of three surviving children born at Blickling Hall in Norfolk. Her brother George and sister Anne were not close to Mary as they grew up and they frequently ganged up against her.

Mary did possess the finest silk dresses and was given an extensive education, so that she could hold the family's high social standing together in public. Her parents had no choice but to provide her with everything she could ever need to find a good wealthy husband.

There are no surviving portraits of Mary but artist Lucas Heron painted a portrait of what he thought the two girls would look like. Mary was always thought to be the fairer of the sisters with light hair and blue eyes.

Mary had a happy childhood at Hever Castle in Kent. However Mary joined the entourage of the Princess Mary Tudor, King Henry VIII's sister, as she prepared to wed Louis XII, the kin of France.

When Mary Tudor returned to England - Louis had died soon after their union - Mary Boleyn stayed in France, spending five years there. She soon became the mistress of King Francis I of France before being passed to other noble men. Francis named her his "English Mare" as he had ridden her many times. She was known as a "very great whore" and was "the most infamous of all".

Mary's parents were said to have developed feelings of dislike towards her because of the effect her behaviour had on the family name. She was appointed lady-in-waiting to Queen Katherine of Aragon and by 1519 her parents and the king had found her a husband, William Carey, who was well respected with royal connections.

In 1522 Mary caught the eye of Henry and as he could take his pick of any lady in his court Mary became his mistress, proving that her beauty must have been compelling.

1524 saw Mary fall pregnant and she gave birth to a girl, followed by a boy in 1526. It is argued that these children, who were conceived whilst she was in a relationship with the king, were his and were branded Royal Bastards. Henry never acknowledged them as his own, even though the boy shared a striking resemblance.

Forever fickle, in 1526 Henry became bored with Mary and set his sights on another prize. Mary's very own sister Anne.

On the 23rd of June 1528 Mary's husband William Carey succumbed to a mysterious sweating sickness, leaving Mary with little to support herself and her two children. Anne even took Mary's youngest child Henry on as her ward and paid for his education to ease the financial strain. However, it took much encouragement for the Boleyn sisters' father to help with the situation.

In 1534 Mary secretly married William Stafford, much to her parents' dismay. William was a mere soldier in the army, a younger son of an Essex landowner, and considered to be much lower than Mary's station. As a result, Anne had her banished from court. Mary then travelled to Calais to spend her days with William whom she married for love.

After Anne's execution, Mary inherited a vast fortune and estates. She is said to have ended her days with her family at Rochford in Essex, passing away from natural causes on 13th July 1543.

4. MARY I, QUEEN OF ENGLAND

It's Thursday, 20th July 1553 – 4.00 p.m.

On the top of a green mound in the sleepy county of Suffolk sits a circular castle topped with red brick chimneys. Its high flint walls and thirteen mighty towers overlook a green wooded park, already hunted for many years. A deep mere surrounded by wetlands lies before the majestic walls, a naturally occurring deterrent to the enemy forces who might consider taking the castle. A deep dry ditch surrounds the curtain walls with bridges leading inside. An army 10,000 strong stands to the north and west inside the park, lines drawn up ready for inspection. Rows of highly polished armour project the summer sun's rays, blinding the sight of the common women, the wives of the infantry showing their allegiance.

A lady, a proclaimed queen, rides aside a white palfrey along the bridge and onto the green pasture. Richly dressed in ruby red velvet, with a silken navy kirtle laying in folds around her legs, a fine white lace peeks above her gown, pleated as a ruff around her thin pale face. Upon her head and sitting snugly behind parted red hair sits a hood in the fashionable French style. The horse nervously sidesteps and rolls her eyes to show the whites in fear. Untrained in battle and scared of the sight ahead she takes a little buck then rears her legs. The queen, a skilled horsewoman, calms her mount and calls her foot soldiers to raise their hands. Holding her tightly corseted tiny waist they assist her to alight as ordered in a gentle practised move. She presents a relaxed, confident air as she walks among the formations. The soldiers bow low to the ground as she inspects them, taking the time to question the leaders.

The infantry handle their pikes, the cavalry their lances and the archers display their arrows upon bended bows. As the sun sits low in the sky, she mounts the now calmly waiting horse and begins her return journey to the safety of Framlingham Castle's walls.

At once and in a thunderous roar, the cavalry advances in a show, a practised move to prove the greatness of Queen Mary's loyal men at arms.

Queen Mary I, known during her five-year reign as Bloody Mary, was the eldest daughter of King Henry VIII and his first wife Catherine of Aragon. She was born on 18th February in the year 1516, one of three surviving children of the royal parents. Mary was well educated by an English tutor, excelled in Latin and was a talented musician. During her childhood she was used as a diplomatic tool by her father who promised her hand in marriage to many potential allies.

In 1525 Mary was sent to Ludlow in the Welsh Marches, the border lands, where she was named Princess of Wales. However, the lack of any surviving official documentation seems to suggest the title was never formalised by her father.

In 1534 Henry VIII broke with Rome, declared himself the head of the Church of England and introduced the Protestant faith to his devout followers. After Henry abandoned Catherine and married Anne Boleyn, Mary's mother was banished to the countryside and Mary was banned from contact. This was an order she dangerously ignored, keeping in touch with her mother via a string of secret letters. Pronounced a bastard and forced to wait on her infant sister Elizabeth, Mary grew further apart from her father.

After Anne Boleyn's fall from grace, Mary's close friend and adviser Eustace Chapuys (the Imperial Ambassador) persuaded her to accept her father's offer of reinstatement to the royal family and the title of princess as long as she agreed to his terms, namely accepting him as the head of the English church and agreeing with his opinion that his marriage to her mother was of an 'incestuous' nature which formally she did. However, Mary privately ignored her father's terms and held Catholic mass within her household, a move that could have seen her in great danger.

In 1544 Mary was accepted back to court and reinstated into the succession after her brother Edward.

1547 saw the death of her father and her brother Edward became king. After direction by those who swayed his decisions, he made English the legal language of the church. At fifteen Edward fell desperately ill with tuberculosis and made his will, cutting out Mary as his heir and naming Lady Jane Grey as his successor to the throne.

Mary, sure of her brother's intent to imprison her, fled to her home at Kenninghall in Norfolk and promptly surrounded herself with her advisors with whom she held council, drawing up plans to regain her rightful place on the throne of England. Whilst she was preparing for the journey to Suffolk, Mary's supporters grew in number and the English noblemen gradually abandoned Lady Jane, making their way to the future queen. One of her supporters, Sir Richard Southwell, marched to her aid with reinforcements of men, stores of provisions and money along with his council and 'long experience'. Receiving confirmation of her brother's death, Mary fled onwards to Framlingham Castle, arriving on Wednesday, 12th July 1553. To her relief she entered the small Suffolk town at 8.00 p.m. finding the streets lined with the local country folk, with the gentry and justices awaiting her in the deer park below the fortress.

On 19th July 1553 Mary received the confirmation that she had been formally declared Queen of England. Mary, the first ever queen in her own right, was thirty-seven "with a sincere and hearty manner". Within days she made her triumphant entry into London where the streets were lined with her people weeping with joy waving banners and streamers above their heads.

It's Thursday, 3rd August 1553

Her grace, upon a white palfrey adorned with embroidered gold cloth right down to its feet, sits confidently. Dressed in a royal purple gown in the French fashion with a kirtle of purple satin, she displays the work of her goldsmiths and with pearls sewn upon her hood. The Mayor of London stands before her, offering a sceptre as a token of his loyalty and homage. Behind her ride her noblemen, one holding her train over his shoulder. Riding on she reaches the Tower where, met with her prisoners she publicly pardons them. Ahead the trumpets sound and the echo of gunfire from the tower guns fills the air. To the joy of her loyal countrymen Mary I, Queen of England has come home.

5. MARY HOWARD

It's Sunday, 26th November 1533

A young girl of no more than fourteen years of age waits impatiently within the Royal Chapel of Hampton Court. She shivers, feeling the cold frosty air through her heavy red velvet gown. Ruby and silver jewels sparkle, catching the light of the many candles dotted around. Finally, a teenage boy takes his place by her side. Her father stands proudly as his arrangement, three years in the making, is officiated. Repeating their vows, the betrothal is complete, the young couple are officially man and wife.

Mary Howard was born in 1519, at Kenninghall, Norfolk. She was the youngest daughter of Thomas and Elizabeth Howard (née Stafford) the 3rd Duke and Duchess of Norfolk and the second most senior nobles in the English peerage.

Elizabeth claimed that after two days and one night in labour, Thomas roughly took her out of bed and proceeded to drag her around the house by her hair. In a letter to Thomas Cromwell he denies this, writing that a scar on her head was several months old.

Mary's first introduction to the dangers of the Tudor court was in 1521 when her grandfather Edward Stafford, Duke of Buckingham, was executed at Tower Hill.

Mary grew up in Norfolk, spending her childhood divided between the Howards' properties in East Anglia. As her older brother Henry was well educated it is most likely she was given an education appropriate to her social standing. She could certainly read the scripture in English and knew some French and she later assisted with the writing of the Devonshire manuscript which contained poems created at court.

Mary is described as having a kind demeanour and was both beautiful and smart, a deadly combination for some in the Tudor court. Her father once said 'she is too wise for a woman and that's why I love her so much'.

When she was ten years old her father and Henry VIII (supposedly pushed by Anne Boleyn) arranged her marriage without a dowry, betrothing her to Henry Fitzroy. Henry was the bastard son of Henry VIII and his mistress Bessie Blount. Born at Ingatestone, Essex, Fitzroy was a well-educated boy recognized by the king and given the title of Duke of Richmond and Somerset. Mary's mother was fiercely against the union and after a blazing row with Anne Boleyn was banished from court.

Katherine, Mary's older sister, was married in 1529, to the Earl of Derby but tragically the union was brief as she died just months later of the much-feared Plague. Mary was devastated.

She joined the court in 1532, attending to Anne Boleyn alongside the other ladies-in-waiting. Anne rewarded her whilst at Windsor castle by declaring her Marquise of Pembroke.

It's Sunday, 26th November 1533

Mary was married to Henry Fitzroy at just fourteen, as the law stated that girls could be married in Tudor times as young as twelve and boys aged fourteen. Love and romance are not considered in an aristocratic marriage. As they were so young, they were not permitted to cohabit after the wedding so both travelled back to their respective homes.

On 22nd July 1536, Anne Boleyn was executed for treason. Just a month later Fitzroy suddenly took to his bed, dangerously ill, displaying symptoms such as fever, headache, and weakness. The cause of his unexpected demise was explained to the court as tuberculosis. Henry was inconsolable and Fitzroy was very quietly and quickly taken and buried at Thetford Priory.

The low-key funeral and speed of the burial was unusual and it was rumoured that the deceased was involved in a conspiracy to strip the king of his throne, putting Fitzroy in his place. This combined with the fact of Jane Seymour's pregnancy (later miscarried) put Fitzroy second in line to the throne with the king then having a legitimate heir. It was certain that the king knew of this plan but did he believe that Fitzroy was heading the plot? Did Fitzroy really die of tuberculosis? That we will never know for sure.

Mary went home. As her parents had separated, she lived with her father on his handouts, but when it became clear that the king was refusing her Jointure (money for marriage) she wrote to Thomas Cromwell pleading her case. The king had decided that as her marriage was never consummated, he did not have to pay the fee. Mary resorted to selling off her land and even her precious collection of jewels in order to make ends meet. She stubbornly continued her argument until the King gave in and paid the fee.

In 1540, Mary from a devoutly Catholic family began to follow the new faith.

In December 1546, her father, the Duke of Norfolk, and her brother were arrested for treason, held at Ely Palace, then imprisoned in the Tower of London. Late one day the commissioners turned up at Kenninghall where they tore the house apart searching for proof of high treason. As they questioned her Mary is said to have been 'sore, perplexed, fumbling and likely to fall down'.

Come January 1547, her brother was found guilty and sentenced to be hung, drawn and quartered but after hearing pleas of the court the King showed mercy and decided on a beheading at Tower Hill.

On 28th January 1547, the legendary King Henry VIII passed away in Whitehall Palace, London. It's not clear how he died but documentary evidence states that it was either smallpox or of the complications of the ulcer obtained in a hunting accident. He was interred at St George's Chapel in Windsor next to his third wife Jane Seymour, the only woman he truly loved.

Thomas Howard, escaping execution by days, was released and sent home to Kenninghall. Mary collected her nieces and nephews and took them home, employing John Foxe as their tutor.

On 7th December 1577, Mary herself passed away. Her death was sudden and unexpected. It's said she died of influenza which was rife among the ladies at court. Mary did not leave a will.

She is buried in a tomb at the church of St Michael the Archangel in Framlingham, next to Henry Fitzroy whose remains had previously been moved due to the dissolution of the priories. Framlingham was chosen as the castle was the official seat of the Howard family.

6. KATHERINE WILLOUGHBY

It's Thursday, 7th September 1533

A girl, slight in frame, brushes a stray red hair from her face, patting it down to re-join her flowing wavy locks. She is dressed in damask edged with velvet and scattered with pearls. The day is bright, breezy and the chapel well-lit by the morning sun. The priest stands, Bible in hand, waiting patiently for the couple to reach the porch. She can feel his presence beside her. Tall and well-built, he walks with his head held high. Dressed in crimson velvet and satin edged with golden thread embroidered in the cloth he looks every way the nobleman. She shudders at the thought of the earlier conversation with the older ladies. Her wifely duty. She cannot shake the confused emotions that run through her mind. Him her protector, her guardian and now to be her husband, not the one intended.

Just a few more steps and it begins. She was born for this moment, trained and moulded into a dutiful wife. Soon it begins, time to make her family proud. To become a duchess. Turning her head to smile at her future husband the couple arrive.

The ring feels heavy on her right hand, the gown tearing at her waist. They kneel at the altar with a cloth over their heads. At once it's removed, it is done; she is a wife. A fourteen-year-old wife, a duchess. She is now a royal, one of the most powerful ladies at court.

Katherine Willoughby was born on 22nd March 1519 at Parham Hall in Suffolk. Her parents were William Willoughby and Maria de Salinas, titled in their own right. They had three children, sadly only one survived. Maria was lady in waiting to Catherine of Aragon and was constantly at her side. Therefore the beautiful young Katherine knew little of her parents.

Tragedy stuck in October 1526 when her father died while on business in Suffolk. He was buried at Mettingham. Katherine, being his only living heir, inherited the barony including sixty manors spread over the kingdom, making her the richest heiress of her time, worth £900 a year. Her mother, unable to parent her child, gave the wardship to Henry VIII.

When she turned ten the King sold her wardship to Charles Brandon the 1st Duke of Suffolk for a jaw-dropping £2,266 13s 4d. With Mary Tudor (the King's sister) and Charles Brandon she found some happiness, living at Westhorpe Hall, Suffolk. Katherine was educated beside Brandon's daughters, Frances and Eleanor, similar in age they became firm friends. Their brother Henry was much younger but had been her betrothed for quite some time. We can only imagine how the young girls must have felt about their annoying little brother marrying their best friend!

On 25th June 1533 at around seven or eight in the morning Mary Tudor, Brandon's true chosen love, passed away, leaving her three children motherless and Katherine feeling quite alone.

Since Mary had been ill for a while, complaining of a searing pain in her side, Brandon was prepared for her death. His next shocking move reminds us that life was all about politics, money and titles within the Tudor court.

A month later, Katherine Willoughby became an orphan, at just fourteen years old when her mother, Maria passed away at court, leaving Catherine of Aragon devastated at losing her closest ally, during the most difficult period of her life.

Just three months after Mary Tudor's funeral (with Katherine as head mourner) the court began whispering, writing letters to their kin. Brandon cancelled his ward's betrothal to Henry, his youngest son, and claimed Katherine as his own. Close to fifty years old and heavily in debt, this move was not just based on lust for a beautiful girl but political. His son was in poor health and could die, and then Katherine's land, title and money would be lost to the family. With his plan he would ease his finances and become the richest duke in court.

Shocking by today's standards, the marriage was a clever match. Katherine, a duchess just as her parents had dreamed, seemed to be happy with the match especially when Henry, her intended, died the following year.

By 1534, Katherine had given birth to a healthy boy named Henry after his godfather the king and with the arrival of a second son Charles in 1537, she felt her family complete, winning a firm position in the royal family. The boys were named as heirs to the throne just after King Henry's own children. At this time the family were ordered to reside in Lincolnshire to control the northern nobles who were well known for their uprisings.

With her wit and sharp tongue Katherine became absorbed in the new Protestant religion. Devoted to learning, she became an outspoken advocate of the English Reformation, bringing her close to the king's attention and affection. They became firm friends, exchanging gifts from 1534, despite her position of lady in waiting to his chosen wives. They spent a lot of time together at court and Henry (who loved to sing and play) attended her masques. These were lavish courtly entertainments. One such game recorded that Katherine had to choose who she would most like and dislike bringing her into dinner, naming the Bishop of Winchester, Stephen Gardiner, as her least favourite man.

She further insulted him by naming her dog Gardiner and the court would howl with laughter when she called him to heel.

The Suffolks were given the honour of welcoming the dowdy Anne of Cleves to these shores in 1539, and much later were chosen to arrange the king's progress with Catherine Howard. Howard was to become famous for her trysts with Thomas Culpeper but always claimed she was on her best behaviour whilst staying with the Brandons.

It was in the court of Catherine Parr where our Katherine began to shine. The girls became firm friends, A poorly educated Catherine hung on every word and the girls became involved in controversial meetings about the Protestant faith, with the queen's opinions becoming dangerously well known. Life continued happily until 22nd August 1545 when, quite unexpectedly, Charles Brandon died in Guildford, surrounded by loved ones. This left twenty-six-year-old Katherine with her lands and wealth as well as being a single mother to her boys. Again, very interestingly, we see a glimpse of Katherine's personality as she makes the very unusual decision to purchase her sons' wardships.

Almost unheard of in these times. She then refuses to arrange their marriages calling the practice a sin before God. Does this move indicate her feelings surrounding her own betrothal and arranged marriage to Brandon at such a young age?

Now, titled, rich and single, rumours in court turn to her future and her friendship with the king, it's said he was ready to put his wife Catherine aside and make Katherine Brandon his next wife, a whisper that angered the king in public and we can assume that being so close to his wife, it would have upset the young women, maybe causing friction in their relationship.

All this gossip was finally quelled when the infamous King Henry VIII died in Whitehall Palace on 28th January 1547, at fifty-five years of age, from natural causes, hastened by his huge appetite for food and an ulcer from an old hunting injury.

Wasting no time his widow Catherine remarried. She and Thomas Seymour were wed in the moonlit gardens of Chelsea Manor House. Again, the rumours indicate that she was pregnant by Henry and desperate to have the child within the confines of marriage. The pregnancy was not an easy one, with the mother's advanced age medical practitioners were worried about her health. In October 1548 a healthy girl, lady Mary was born, much to the delight of her father. But this moment of celebration was cut short when just six days later Catherine succumbed to puerperal fever.

It's Tuesday, 7th September 1548

Wrapped and chested in lead, the corpse remains in the privy chamber whilst things are made ready.

Katherine Brandon, face swollen and sodden with tears stands by her stool waiting, thinking. She sees the coffin draped with black cloth and garnished with escutcheons of marriages, that of her and King Henry in pale, under the crown, and that of her and Thomas Seymour, also in pale but without a crown. She looks around searching the faces but the widowed Thomas, much grieved, was nowhere to be seen.

First the hooded conductors shrouded in black cloaks with blackened staves in hand. She hangs her head as the tears fall, so big, so many, wetting her dress. Unaware of the scene, the choir begin to sing in English, a slight smile forms on her face as she considers what would have been her friend's excitement at this.

As the coffin is lowered into the cold ground the choir sing a Te Deum. In English. She chuckles.

Just six months later the tiny Lady Mary Seymour becomes an orphan as her father is executed for treason. His will gave instructions that Katherine was to become her guardian. We know from the documents that she was very unhappy about this. I wonder if she blamed the child for the death of her friend. Within two years Mary must also have died as she never gets mentioned again.

As Katherine felt she could take no more, her precious boys, students at Cambridge, succumb to the sweating sickness despite fleeing to Lincolnshire. Within hours of each other they are gone forever. There is still no modern label for this mysterious contagious disease. It's made clear just how devastated she is in a letter to Sir William Cecil where she writes how she felt it was God's way, a punishment for all her sins and how her religion would see her through these dark times.

A year later she marries for love. Her bridegroom is her Gentleman Usher Richard Bertie, a marriage much beneath her station, and she later gives birth to a baby girl, Susan. But during this time King Edward VI tragically dies and Mary I seizes the throne, turning the country on its head by reintroducing the Catholic faith, executing and burning anyone in her way. With Stephen Gardiner (Katherine's enemy) as Lord Chancellor the Berties collect their belongings and escape to Europe. They welcome a fourth child Peregrine in Wesel, whilst on the run from the vicious queen. In 1558, Queen Mary dies, Elizabeth comes to the throne and a new era of peace and Protestant faith ensues. This paves the way for Katherine's return.

With her lands restored, the family returned to their duties. Katherine visited other nobles, heard petitions and supported her people by giving favours and aid, picking priests for the local churches and distributing Bibles. Her final years were spent happily as a family with Richard and the children. She died on 19th September 1580 at Spilsby and was buried there three days later.

7. LADY JANE GREY

It's Wednesday, 9th July 1553

A teenage girl straightens her back, easing her pony through the gates of Syon House, situated in the west of the vast city of London. She is a slight girl with long, plaited, reddish hair. Her face is freckled, standing out from her delicate pale skin, making her look even more beautiful as well as portraying an air of innocence and sweetness only reserved for the young.

She dismounts, falling into a strong man's arms as he eases her carefully onto her feet so gently it was as if he was carrying the most precious jewels. She has been called to London via a messenger with very little explanation of why she was required to make haste.

Waving the man away she sets about adjusting her gown, smoothing the creases as best as she can with her tiny elegant hands. She straightens her headdress, standing tall, not forgetting to raise her chin and present herself as her mother has trained her to from birth. As she surveyed the scene before her, two gentlemen hurried through the yard, dropping to their knees and gently raising her hand to brush against their damp lips, one after the other. The girl, embarrassed, could do little to hide the redness of her cheeks as the men (confusing her even further) greeted her calling her their "Sovereign Lady." Thinking in a calm and rational fashion, she concluded the men must be mistaken as King Edward VI was still very much alive. Were they playing a cruel and dangerous trick to gauge her response then no doubt report that to the council?

The girl, Lady Jane, was then led to the Chamber of State and informed of the devastating news that King Edward had sickened and died. Her calm demeanour reducing, her mind whirled with so many questions; When did he die? How do the people not know this? Why was she not informed sooner? Head spinning, she swayed scrabbling for a chair. Something, anything solid and still. Through her tears she cried "Such a noble Prince."

When she was quite recovered, her parents knelt, paying homage to her. Now it all began to make sense. Her family had manoeuvred her, step by step, into a position she desperately disfavoured. Protesting fervently, she declared to all in the room that the crown was not her right and "pleaseth me not," stating that the Lady Mary was the rightful heir. At once both her mother and husband demanded she obey them, and very reluctantly she obeyed, still insisting she was not right for the role. As the evening came to an end she retired to bed. When she left her chamber the following morning, she was adorned in Tudor green and white with raised chopines three inches high (these were heeled shoes) and looking every inch a queen whilst Guildford, her husband, was radiant in pure white and golden cloth.

Lady Jane Grey was born in 1537, to noble parents Henry Grey, Duke of Suffolk and Frances Brandon, Duchess of Suffolk who was a niece of Henry VIII. Jane was the oldest of three with two sisters, Katherine born 1540 and Mary born 1545. As was the custom Jane (named after Jane Seymour, Prince Edward's mother) was baptised within forty-eight hours in the parish church at Bradgate, Leicestershire.

Jane's parents were very strict, beatings were frequent and an answer to most of her parents' challenges in bringing up three young girls. Jane did not exactly have a happy childhood but she was exceptionally bright and was granted the best education money could buy. Therefore she found comfort in her learning, mastering Greek and Latin at a young age and later adding French, Hebrew and Italian to her repertoire. She also benefited under the tutelage of her father's chaplain, John Aylmer. John became very fond of Jane and it was rumoured that he had fallen deeply in love with her during their time together.

In 1546, at just nine years old Jane escaped her parents' discipline and went to live with the kindly Catherine Parr and her fourth husband Thomas Seymour of Sudley. Jane adored Catherine as many others did, she filled the gap of a loving mother Jane had never experienced before. When Catherine gave birth to Lady Mary in 1548 (the unexpected but very much wanted child) there was much joy but it was short-lived as just six days later Catherine succumbed to childbed fever. Devastated and uncertain of her future, young Jane was chief mourner at the lavish funeral.

Lady Jane became the ward of Thomas Seymour who wasted no time in attempting to arrange a marriage with Edward VI. However, when Edward contracted measles and began to spit up blood it became clear that he would not live for much longer, resulting in a hurriedly drawn up contract naming Lady Jane as successor to the throne above the declared bastards Elizabeth and Mary Tudor, who was also avoided due to her strong Catholic faith. Just months later Thomas was arrested for high treason and executed; his young daughter Lady Mary then fizzled away from the written history, never to be mentioned again.

In 1553, Lady Jane was under the wardship of John Dudley, Duke of Northumberland, and was subjected to being bullied into marrying the complete stranger Lord Guilford Dudley in a hurried private ceremony at Northumberland's London residence, Durham Place. The ceremony was shared with her sister Katherine and Guilford's sister Catherine Dudley. The triple wedding was such a sudden event that the girls were forced to borrow clothing from the royal Master of the Wardrobe. Jane shone, wearing a gown of gold and silver brocade embroidered with glittering diamonds and pink and cream pearls which caught the light as she moved. Jane was so innocent she could not even have fathomed the lengths John Dudley would be prepared go to. His plan was to place Jane firmly on the throne with his son Guilford seated next to her as King of England.

As if paving the way for this plan, Edward VI died on 6th July 1553. Jane was informed two days later whilst being forced to accept the crown by her husband and parents.

On Thursday 19th between three and four o'clock in the afternoon Jane was taken in a parade of barges to the Tower of London to collect the crown jewels but the public did not cheer, they did not clap and smile, no one called her name with glee. They had just found out that their king had died and now they had to accept some strange unknown cousin as queen. After a lavish traditional welcome Lady Jane Grey entered the Tower without the knowledge that she would never leave the great fortress again. Once inside she was taken to the Presence Chamber where they sat her under the state canopy. Once again Jane tried to object, stating that she never wanted the crown, but she was manipulated to simply try it on to see if it fitted and thus the unwanted title was hers, Lady Jane Grey had been crowned. She was now queen. However reluctant she was, when Guilford stated that, as her husband, she was to declare him king, she refused, leaving him running to his mother in tears. In a united front they both tormented Jane for over an hour but she stood by her decision.

Between 11th and 13th July, it is speculated that Jane was ill. She suspected the Duchess of Northumberland of slowly poisoning her as all the skin peeled off of her back. Whether this was a result of anxiety or she was indeed being poisoned we will never know.

By 15th the small royal party were in serious trouble. The people would not support Jane and called for Mary, joining her troops as they marched towards London. The council decided to send Jane's father to lead the royal troops despite Jane protesting about his failing health and advanced age. Jane exhausted, swollen and red-faced from constantly crying, was deserted by her council and on 19th July 1553, Mary was crowned Queen of England in Cheapside as the church bells rang and people cheered and rejoiced in the streets. Jane was removed from her rooms to less elegant surroundings above those of deputy lieutenant Thomas Brydges where she stayed until she was relocated to the cottage on Tower Green. She was kept in comfort with an allowance and allowed to walk within the confines of the Tower.

On 27th July Jane's father was arrested for treason and imprisoned and whilst Jane begged the queen for a pardon for her husband it became clear that her mother would be making no effort to save Jane herself.

On 14th November 1553 Jane pleaded guilty and was sentenced to death for high treason. Just eleven days later Jane's father was executed and, on 12th February 1554, watching from the Tower window Jane insisted on observing her husband's execution. Next at 10.00 a.m. Jane was led out of the tower. Climbing the hill, she passed the cart containing his dead body. Dressed all in black, she made a speech, gave her handkerchief to Elizabeth Tilney and her prayer book to Thomas Brydges, removed her gown, head dress and collar and tossed her hair out of the way. She was then blindfolded and after slightly losing her composure when she could not find the block without assistance, she laid down her head and in one swing of the axe Lady Jane Grey was executed.

CHAPTER TWO

INFLUENTIAL WOMEN

1. BOUDICCA

It's ante diem VII Idus Maias (9th May)

A tall slim woman crowned by waist-length reddish hair stands proudly upon a chariot surrounded by wicker panels. Beside (but slightly to her rear) stand two young girls, no more than twelve years old. They share their mother's tawny hair and piercing eyes. She wears a colourful woollen dress with a cloak around her shoulders fixed upon her breast by a golden and bejewelled brooch. She wears a thick torc around her neck, a symbol of her royalty. A symbol of a queen. With her long sword in her hand, she gestures toward the heavens, waving and pointing the weapon as she delivers an inspired speech to the 100,000 strong tattooed tribesmen before her. She releases a hare, its direction a signal from the gods. The woman reminds the men that they are not only fighting for a cause before the eyes of all Britons, but for the deities who are always on their side. That heaven is always on the side of the righteous. She declares "I'm not just a woman descended from noble ancestry before you, I'm one of you. I am avenging our lost freedom." She turns her chariot and begins the march to Camulodunum (Colchester).

Boudicca was born around AD 30 into a wealthy elite family in Deodford (Thetford). As a child she was trained in the art of warcraft, becoming a ferocious fighter equal to any tribesman. As a lady, she was also taught how to behave in social situations and how to be a good wife and mother.

In AD 43, Emperor Claudius of Rome invaded and settled in Britain. He offered a few native tribes (the Iceni being one) the option of being a client kingdom. This granted tribesmen the right to keep their lands and for the king to govern his people as he saw fit, the caveat being that the tribes were now loyal allies of Rome and required to pay taxes for the privilege. The Iceni people were considered an organized society. Being both wealthy and powerful they minted their own coins and had a sophisticated economy. They shunned the Roman lifestyle, preferring their own rich cultural heritage. Some of the finest archaeological artefacts come from Iron Age hoards.

At the age of eighteen, Boudicca married the ruler of the Iceni, King Prasutagas, who ruled over all the land now known as Norfolk and Suffolk. She welcomed two strong and healthy girls into their family upon whom she showered all her love and affection. Both children were well educated and they too were taught the art of warcraft, growing up to be quite the little warriors. The family lived in relative peace with small skirmishes breaking out between neighbouring tribes. One such event occurred in AD 47. The ruling governor had ordered the Iceni to disarm, they refused and discontentment began to build.

Upon Prasutaga's death in AD 60 a will was wisely left behind. In it, half of the kingdom was left to his daughters and half to Emperor Nero in Rome to settle a debt. This request was totally ignored by Nero, who sent the imperial procurator Catus Decianus to seize the entire estate and the lands of other noble Iceni tribesmen, taking away their ally status. This move left the tribe slaves of the Roman Empire. Boudicca furiously stormed to meet someone with a higher authority than Catus and she complained about the situation, A deadly mistake, as Nero had stated that any resistance would be treated as an act of rebellion.

Now she was under Roman rule and the soldiers tied her up in the centre of the town and publicly whipped her, using a weapon with protruding metal spikes and thick leather knots to increase her pain. Unfortunately, they did not leave it there. The evil sickening men took turns raping Boudicca's two young girls, forcing her to watch. This barbaric act was a sacrilegious insult to her, the tribe and their gods. Under Roman law it was forbidden to have sexual relations with a widow so Boudicca avoided being sexually attacked by the group. During these times daughters of disgraced consuls were habitually raped. Executioners commonly deflowered virgins before they carried out the sentence because of a fear of offending their gods.

In a fit of furious anger and to avenge her young daughters Boudicca began to form an army. She invited the leaders of the Trinovantes, the Cornovii and the Durotiges to join the revolt, amassing an army of 100,000 highly trained warriors armed and ready to kill. Boudicca saw her chance when Gaius Suetonius Paulinus (the Roman Governor) marched on Anglesey, Wales leaving Camulodunum undefended. A firestorm march through the East of England saw Roman settlements burnt and their owners slaughtered. On arriving at the Roman stronghold, finding it defended only by elderly soldiers, the army took Camulodunum, burning everything in sight and looting and ransacking the town. Once at the great temple Boudicca severed the head from the statue of the Emperor Nero, throwing it into the river Alde. The ancient Britons had a ritual of drowning severed heads. I believe this act was to show that the tribal customs would go on despite Roman interference.

Camulodunum destroyed, she headed for Londinium (London).

Suetonius, hearing of the mass slaughter, began to march his legion back from Wales and arrived in Londinium before the tribes. However, instead of fighting with so few men, he evacuated the city and turned and ran, abandoning the city to the rebels. Once Boudicca's army arrived, they killed and tortured anyone who had stayed inside the city.

The Britons were a fierce enemy who liked to keep trophies from their victims, decapitating them and keeping the heads. They were a gang of bloodthirsty barbarians who were known to hang women upside down, cut off their breasts and sew them to their mouths (giving the impression they were being eaten) and then impaling them on sharp skewers. Armed with either the axe or long sword the warriors were heavily tattooed and covered in body paint and it's well documented that they fought naked.

Next in store for the brutal revenge was Verulamium (St Albans) where, as in the two battles before, the army burnt the city to the ground, torturing and murdering anyone in sight. Suetonius again refused to defend any of the population who refused to leave before the warriors' arrival.

Between 70,000 and 80,000 people were slaughtered between the three settlements and Nero was tempted to withdraw his troops from Britain altogether. As they marched the army grew and grew, yet time was ticking for Boudicca and her revolt. They took no prisoners but mutilated the inhabitants with wanton rituals.

Suetonius now had the time to regroup, gathering together 10,000 men and choosing the perfect battle site, most likely in the West Midlands near Watling Street, the Roman road. The waiting Roman army were placed with the legions in the centre, auxiliary foot soldiers on the flank and the cavalry on each side.

The Britons arrived wearing opiate face paint to prevent fatigue and fear. Weapons in hand they formed a wedge. However not accustomed to such battles they made a fatal mistake, positioning the wagons which housed their women and children behind them and thus leaving no space to retreat.

Tacitus records Boudicca addressing her troops standing tall upon her chariot with her daughters ready to avenge them. In her speech she is quoted as saying she is not only avenging 'my scourged body, the outraged chastity of my daughters. Roman lust has gone so far that not our very person, nor even age or virginity are left unpolluted. ... This is a woman's resolve; as for men, they may live and be slaves.' The battle-ready queen made it clear she would win or else she would die. Boudicca's force, now 230,000 strong, were armed with swords, spears and knives. Men, woman and children stood battle ready and Boudicca led them onto the site in a tightly packed mass. The Romans let loose their javelins, killing many then marching forward in wedge formation. The auxiliaries and cavalry attacked and broke into the rebel ranks. Once they had broken through to the rear, the Roman army murdered the women and children. The better trained and equipped Romans massacred the Britons, leaving this battle the bloodiest seen on British soil. The Romans had won, losing just a few hundred men.

Thanks to the published works of Publius Cornelius Tacitus (Life of Agricola and The Annals) and Lucius Cassius Dio (The Rebellion of Boudicca) Boudicca's' exploits have been recorded, thus enabling others to learn her story and bring her back to life by writing her biography for us to remember her as the fierce warrior she was who struggled to bring freedom to her people.

It's here that Cassius Dio and Tacitus differ on their version of history. Dio claims that Boudicca fell violently ill after the battle and passed away but Tacitus writes that fearing the wrath of the Romans had she been captured, she poisoned herself. There are no documents which explain the fate of the two girls.

After this event the Britons tried a few uprisings but none gained support like the warrior queen. The Romans went on to rule our Island for many years, withdrawing in around AD 410.

Boudicca went on to be forgotten in the blizzard of history until 1360 when Tacitus' Annals were found.

This was surely a violent uprising and this rebellion ultimately failed but Boudicca earned her place in history as a heroine of our East Anglian ancestors. A woman. A warrior showing exactly what a mother would do for her children.

When you next visit Colchester take the time to visit The George Hotel at 116 High Street. If you asked very politely, they may take you down into the basements where you can see a layer of red burnt clay. Evidence of the slaughter led by Queen Boudicca.

Prince Albert honoured the queen in 1856 by commissioning a bronze statue of her driving a war chariot wielding a spear with her two daughters. It was finally erected in 1902 and you can find it close to Westminster Bridge.

2. ELIZABETH GARRETT ANDERSON

It's Monday, 31st January 1859

A woman dressed in a fine yellow silk gown sits listening to a lecture. She inclines her head as she feels the mounting excitement of the private audience ahead with the famous first female doctor from the United States.

Inspired, she awaits Elizabeth Blackwell MD, holding out her delicate pale hand as the older woman approaches. After some conversation

Blackwell, visibly impressed, studies the bright intelligent lady before her. She feels a surging sense of pride at the fact that she has clearly aroused the young lady's interest into the study of medicine.

The younger woman bade Blackwell good day, feeling quite overwhelmed by the rowdy American's enthusiasm yet a fire had ignited in her, a small intrusive thought that yes, she could. No! Yes, she will.

Elizabeth Garrett Anderson was born on 9th June 1836 at 1 Commercial Road, Whitechapel, London. Her father Newson Garrett was a pawnbroker and a hard worker. Her mother Louisa Dunnell Garrett, a traditional Victorian housewife, educated her ten children at home until Newson earned enough money to move to Aldeburgh and buy a barley and coal merchants at Snape Bridge where he built Snape Maltings.

This change in fortune enabled the family to employ a governess (whom Elizabeth hated) and later Newton would send his eldest girls to a boarding school for young ladies in Blackheath which was for the daughters of gentlemen. Elizabeth challenged her tutors and later in life she shuddered whilst recalling 'the stupidity of the teachers' and a lack of science and maths education.

In 1850 the family, now wealthy enough to run with the upper class, built Alde House and sent Elizabeth on a tour abroad. She then spent the following years living the life of a lady. However, Elizabeth continued her education learning maths, Latin and the sciences to keep her mind sharp.

In 1854 Elizabeth met Emily Davies, a feminist, and the two became firm friends. Emily encouraged her to become a career woman and to reject the socially expected life of an upper-class Victorian lady.

It was five years later during a visit to her sister in London while attending a series of three lectures that Elizabeth met Elizabeth Blackwell who encouraged her to train in medicine. Blackwell, the first female doctor to be added to the medical register, inspired Elizabeth, who arriving home in Suffolk sought her father's approval much to initial disgust. Her mother thought it such a disgrace that it would kill her. However, her parents were always pushing their children to seek success and after much persuasion they agreed to her goal and promised to support her both financially and emotionally throughout her journey.

So Elizabeth's battle to study medicine began. Her father accompanied her to visit several top physicians who each in turn thought it useless to pursue her education if she could never be listed on the medical register. It was on these visits that her father introduced her to Dr William Hawes who agreed to allow Elizabeth a short trial as a nurse at the Middlesex Hospital. This just fed the flame and encouraged her even further. Employing a private tutor, Elizabeth learnt anatomy and physiology three times a week. After her trial as a nurse, she sent an application through to become a student but was rejected. Not one to ever give up, Elizabeth stayed on unofficially as a guest. She learnt the skills of a medical student, attending patients on the wards, working in the dispensary and going to lectures. Unfortunately, that enthusiasm got the wrong kind of attention and following her examinations the all-male students set up a petition claiming that Elizabeth interfered with their progress. So in July 1861 she left the hospital with a certificate of honours in chemistry and privately passed her anatomy and physiology course. By then Elizabeth was determined to get her name on the medical register.

Rejected by Cambridge, Oxford and the University of London, Elizabeth spotted a loophole and pursued a degree with the Licentiate of the Society of Apothecaries. After five years of instruction, she presented her qualifications yet she was struck another blow when they refused her permission to sit the final exams. Her father was outraged and threatened to sue the society who eventually backtracked and allowed her the opportunity. She passed with flying colours and just one year later became the first British woman in history to be listed on the medical register.

In 1865 Elizabeth was living at 20 Upper Berkley Street, London when she set up in practice and in 1866 she moved to 69 Seymour Place where she opened the St. Mary's Dispensary for Women and Children. The public were reluctant to seek a woman for their medical issues but an outbreak of cholera soon changed their opinions and both rich and poor alike rushed to the clinic. In her first year Elizabeth treated 3,000 patients.

The same year Elizabeth and her friend Emily produced a petition signed by 1,500 people for women who were the head of their households to be given the right to vote.

That year, Garrett Anderson joined the first British Women's Suffrage Committee and became a member of the Central Committee of the National Society for Women's Suffrage.

Elizabeth still longed to achieve her dream of a medical degree so she travelled to Paris where women were allowed to train and by 1870, she finally got her medical degree.

The remarkable woman inspired more women when in 1871 she married James George Skelton Anderson, proving that women could marry and have a degree unlike many before her. Even after she welcomed her first child Louisa to the world in 1873, Elizabeth continued to juggle full-time work and a family.

1874 saw her proving that fact again when after the birth of her second daughter Margaret she became the president of the East Anglian branch of the British Medical Association. The same year Elizabeth established the London Medical College for Women where she continued to teach for the next twenty-three years.

Sadly, the happy family was devastated in 1875 when Margaret died from meningitis. Alan her third and final child was born in 1877.

As her husband's health began to falter, he and Elizabeth moved home to Aldeburgh where she spent the final year of her mother's life by her side. The family moved into Alde house in 1903 and enjoyed the last years of her husband's life. He died in 1907.

Elizabeth, never one for a dull life, began to bury herself in politics. With her ferocious intellect and strong desire to make a difference she travelled with suffragette Annie Kenney giving lectures on women's rights. A year later she was voted in as mayor of Aldeburgh, a role her father had also secured before her. During her political years Elizabeth stormed the House of Lords and participated in the Black Friday Riots.

On 17th December 1917 Elizabeth Garrett Anderson died. She is remembered in Ipswich where the hospital emergency department bears her name. Sadly, she never got to witness all women obtaining the right to vote, despite spending her life championing women's rights.

3. EDITH CAVELL

It's Tuesday, 12th October 1915

A slight pale woman stands before sixteen armed men holding Gewehr 88 rifles, each one aimed towards the ash pale yet still smiling woman before them. The German Chaplain beside her clasps her fragile hand and delivers a blessing in English. She turns as a bandage is tied, obscuring her vision from the squad chosen for the brutal task. A sharp word of command swiftly followed by two volleys ring out in perfect unison. The woman slumps to the ground whilst her life slips into the history of a nation at war.

Edith Louisa Cavell was born on 4th December 1865 in Swardeston, Norfolk to Louisa Sophia née Warming and the Reverend Frederick Cavell.

Educated firstly at home, Edith was taught to live by the Anglican faith of her parents to share with those less fortunate and in 1881 she spent several months at Norwich High School for girls in Theatre Street within the city and then attended boarding schools in London, Clevedon (near Bristol) and Peterborough between the ages of 16 and 19. During her free time she loved to ice-skate at the moat surrounding the old rectory. She also loved to sketch, becoming quite a talented artist. Several local families boast a painting from Edith's own nimble hands.

She even raised funds for the growing Sunday school by selling cards adorned with her work, mostly depicting wild flowers she had sketched upon the common. She also taught the children in the new school, constructed in 1877, assisting her father in his calling.

In 1884 she began working as a governess, first to a family in Steeple Bumpstead, Essex where she was fondly known for her kindness, her constant happy demeanour. She was always one for fun.

By 1890 she secured a position in Belgium working for the François family in Brussels and staying for five years where she continued to paint and became fluent in French. During her frequent trips back home, she fell in love with her second cousin Eddie Cavell. However, he did not propose due to a chronic health condition which he did not want to trouble her with.

In 1895 father Frederick became seriously ill and Edith returned home to care for him. It was there that she found a true passion for nursing and secured a trial job at Fountains Fever Hospital, Tooting. In 1896 she applied for the role of Nurse Probationer at London Hospital under the Matron Eva Luckes, which she was accepted for. A year later she was sent to Maidstone, Kent during a typhoid outbreak, earning a medal for her life-saving work. Between 1898 and 1903 she climbed the nursing ranks, becoming Assistant Matron at the Shoreditch Infirmary, London.

1907 saw Edith recruited by Dr Antoine Depage as Matron for a pioneer training school for lay nurses, L'École Belge d'Infirmières Diplômées, on the outskirts of Brussels. By 1910 she was mentor for thirteen kindergartens, twenty-four schools of nursing and three hospitals whilst holding three lectures a week for medical professionals and nursing her close friends' morphine-addicted daughter.

It was on one of Edith's trips back home to her widowed mother in College Road, Norwich when her life stood at the crossroads. Whilst weeding in the garden she heard the news of the German invasion of Belgium. To her mother (as she cut her visit short) she is remembered to have said "At a time like this I am needed more than ever".

On returning to her clinic, she was to nurse the victims of war and had no qualms about treating both allied and enemy soldiers with the same loving care shown as always. When Brussels fell, the enemy claimed her institution as their own, many of the staff left but Edith stayed on under the close eye of the Germans who regularly searched the premises.

In the autumn of 1914 two stranded British soldiers found their way to the training school where they were given refuge. Others followed, all of them spirited away to the neutral safety of Holland. One such occasion saw Edith meeting a local lad Private Arthur Wood to whom she gave a bible to deliver with letters to her mother. Quickly an underground lifeline was established. Knowing they could all be shot for their work the members continued to provide food and clothing with a passage to safety for up to two hundred allied soldiers using the password "Yorc". However, with up to 6,000 German spies inside Brussels it was only a matter of time until word got out to the wrong people.

On 4th August 1915, five German soldiers and members of the local police broke through the door of the clinic. Tearing the bandages from her hand they struck her in the face and, whilst she was on the ground, they dragged her to a waiting van. Edith was taken to be questioned where she admitted everything having always said "never tell a lie". Trying desperately to keep the arrest a secret it took three weeks for the news to reach the UK by which time her trial had already been held with charges of treason and a verdict of guilty reached. The punishment for such a crime was death.

After ten weeks in St Gilles prison (two of which were in solitary confinement) the desperate attempts at official communication failed with Germany adamant that they were following the law whilst withholding information from those who desperately tried to save Edith's life.

At 2.00 a.m. on Tuesday, 12th October after being driven to the Tir National (the national shooting range) in a black prison van Edith Cavell was executed by firing squad and her body hastily buried within the prison grounds.

The story was used by allied forces as wartime propaganda, making Edith a martyr and the Germans monsters. Recruiting in the UK doubled in the two months following her death.

In 1917 funds raised by two newspapers were used to build six rest homes for nurses in England. Today work still goes on under the Cavell Nurses' Trust.

In May 1919 after being exhumed, Edith's body was transported from Dover to Westminster where a service was held in her honour. She was then escorted to Norwich where she is buried in a spot named Life's Green outside the cathedral.

The lady who saw herself as "Just a nurse doing her duty" bravely rescued two hundred English soldiers with another 2,000 escaping via secret networks such as her own.

4. FLORA SANDES

It's Tuesday, 12th September 1916

A woman dressed in a grey uniform shivers in an icy shallow pit on the crest of a snow-covered hill. She is wearing the official greyish, blue horizon uniform and an indented cap bearing the Serbian coat of arms. With her short cropped grey hair and unfurrowed face there is no doubt she is a woman amongst powerfully built men, her comrades. She has spent the night drifting in and out of a shallow sleep waiting for the order to break cover and charge. Finally, at 7.00 a.m. the order comes and within seconds she is up and running as fast as her legs will carry her through the drifting snow. As she approaches the enemy trench a well-aimed grenade explodes on the ground sending shrapnel shattering about. She falls to the ground a mass of torn flesh and shattered bone.

Flora Sandes was born in Poppleton in Yorkshire on 22nd January 1876 to the Reverend Samuel and Sophia Julia Sandes (née Besnard).

Educated first by a governess and later at finishing school, Flora never found comfort in the life she was expected to lead as a middle-class country lady and once said "I used to pray every night, I might wake up in the morning and find myself a boy". The family moved to Marlesford in Suffolk when she was four where she spent her days riding, shooting and racing about in her classic French sports car.

After travelling the globe and working as a secretary she joined the Ambulance Service and eight days after the outbreak of the Great War she was posted to Serbia to assist doctors in treating the wounded. She nursed the locals during an outbreak of spotted typhus where twenty-one doctors had died in the first month. Contracting the disease herself she was nursed back to life by an Austrian prisoner of war.

In November 1915 during a particularly harsh winter retreat, desperate to serve in a combat role she put on the uniform of a dead soldier, shouldered her rifle and marched with the regiment. After replacing their uniforms in Corfu, the Serbians marched to Salonika where a special ceremony was held formally receiving Flora into the Serbian army. Rising in the ranks to a sergeant her squad was known for doing more work under her than any other. Flora bravely joined her fellow soldiers on the front fighting for their country. She was labelled by her men as their "Nasa Engleskinja" (Our Englishwoman) and by the British press as their "Joan of Arc". She was often seen smoking and drinking with her men. For them it was not strange for a woman for join the Serbian Army as numbers were so few they were accepted on their own merits.

After being wounded at the Battle of Monastir in Macedonia she was rescued by her men and given a bottle of brandy and a cigarette on the way to hospital. She was injured in twenty-four places with her right side torn from shoulder to knee. At her bedside by the request of the Prince Regent she was awarded the rare gold and silver cross of the Kara George Star (the Order of Karađorđe's Star) for bravery in the field, the highest Serbian military award. Flora remained in hospital for some months as the only female inmate amongst 1,600 men. Once nursed back to health she was offered a "cushy billet" which she declined. Flora was injured once more, ending up in a Serbian Relief Camp in Tunisia.

She remained with her men in their last great drive breaking the Bulgarian army and recovering Serbia for the people.

Once the war had finished Flora had reached the rank of Serjeant Major of the 2nd Serbian Army Corps.

After demobilisation she settled in Belgrade but never enjoyed civilian life.

In 1927 she married Yuri Yudenitch a Colonel in the White Russian Army; the happy couple settled in Yugoslavia until April, 1941 when the Nazis attacked. Flora, now 65, donned her uniform and marched to fight. After eleven days she and Yuri were incarcerated by the Gestapo and once released, they had to report in once a week.

Two months later Yuri sadly passed away from heart failure. Flora, now alone, made her way to Jerusalem then onto Rhodesia (Zimbabwe) where she was the centre of gossip, having been witnessed drinking and smoking with the black peasant community.

In 1946 the Adriatic mission assisted her return to Suffolk. Later wheelchair-bound she was often seen pelting at full speed between the local villages with the wind in her hair.

In November, 1956 Flora died at Ipswich Hospital having just renewed her passport. She is remembered on a plaque at St Andrew's Church, Marlesford, Suffolk.

Lieutenant Colonel Flora Sandes-Yudenich demonstrated that women of any age can do anything they put their minds to.

5. VIOLET JESSOP

It's Sunday, 14th April 1912 - 23.30h

A weary stewardess undresses and falls into bed. Just ten minutes later as sleep began to claim her a loud screech and violent rumble raises her from her bed. Redressing quickly, she heads up on deck.

Violet Constance Jessop was born on 1st October 1887 in Argentina, close to Bahia Blanca. She was the first of nine children born to Irish immigrants, William and Katherine.

As a child she contracted tuberculosis and doctors prepared her family for an untimely death. But for the first time of many, luck was on her side.

Violet was described as short, bright-eyed with an engaging direct manner.

In 1905, at Mendoza, Argentina her father sadly died in hospital upon the operating table. As a result, Violet and her family moved back to England where she attended a French convent school in Kent.

Later for financial reasons she came home, and while her mother went to sea as a stewardess, Violet cared for her younger siblings.

Following in Katherine's footsteps by 1908, Violet became a stewardess for the Royal Mail Line beginning her lifelong career at sea, serving on the Orinoco, the Majestic, the Adriatic and the Oceanic.

On 20th September 1911, she was on board the RMS (Royal Mail Ship) Olympic when it collided with HMS Hawke. Thankfully the ship managed to limp ashore resulting in all the passengers' survival.

Staying with the White Star line Violet was given the opportunity to work in first-class on board the unsinkable Titanic during her maiden voyage to New York.

It's 14th April 1912 - 23.40h

Titanic has hit an iceberg and the order is given to fill the lifeboats.

Violet was assisting women and children on deck climb into the waiting lifeboats when she was handed a small child and ordered into Lifeboat 16.

The survivors sat frozen as they watched the ship going down killing over 1,500 staff and passengers on-board.

The next morning, she was picked up by the RMS Carpathia where she and the remaining passengers were taken on to New York.

By June 1912, the brave Violet Jessop re-joined the Olympic where she stayed until war broke out when she joined the Merchant Navy. Going ashore she began to train as a VAD (Voluntary Aid Detachment) nurse for the British Red Cross.

After training she was sent to serve on a hospital ship nursing injured servicemen aboard HMHS (His Majesty's Hospital Ship) Britannic, sister ship to Olympic and Titanic.

On the morning of 21st November 1916, whilst in the Aegean Sea off the coast of the Greek island of Kea, her ship struck a sea mine. With all portholes open for ventilation, she quickly began to take on water.

While most of the lifeboats got clear, Violet's was floating dangerously close to the still-running propellers. The boat was pulled so close she hit her head on the keel and had to be pulled back into the lifeboat.

Over 1,000 people were rescued but tragically thirty people died that day.

In late October 1923, Violet was married to John James Lewis in Brentford, Essex, although this union was very brief.

At the age of sixty-three in December 1950 she signed off her life at sea and began her retirement in Great Ashfield, Bury St Edmunds, Suffolk.

On 5th May 1971 Violet, still wearing a wig from her head wound, passed away from congenital heart failure.

Violet Constance Jessop is buried close to her family at Hartest.

In 1996, her memoirs entitled Titanic Survived were published.

"Death waits for no man but it waited for Violet Jessop".

6. ELSIE TILNEY

It's Sunday, 23rd July 1939

A well-dressed woman sporting a smart grey skirt and matching jacket boards the train to Paris. In her arms she holds a baby girl tightly to her chest as if she fears she may be snatched from her safety at any moment.

As she struggles to wrestle her case into the section above, she stops as if to consider, and decides to rest the girl in the window seat while she quickly stashes her case in the compartment. Within seconds she has reclaimed the child into her embrace where she stays for the entire journey back home.

At the station a solitary man with a nervous demeanour waits for the train. He scans the crowds, watching the men in uniform dotted around. As the train arrives the woman spies the man and hurries to his side at once, releasing the child in to her waiting father's strongly muscled grasp. The nervous couple quickly say farewell and split up, leaving the station in haste to return home. The lady feels a strong sense of relief as she travels back to her lodgings, she did it, she rescued the child and returned her to her Jewish family. They would spend the war in hiding, protecting their child at all costs.

Elsie Maude Tilney was born at 21 Carlyle Road, West Wymer, Norwich on 3rd October, 1893 to Albert Joseph and Hannah Rachel Tilney née Chapman. Elsie was one of five children who in the 1901 census lived at 95 Gloucester Street in Heigham and her father is listed as a stationer's clerk.

In 1903 Elsie became a member of the Surrey Chapel at 2-6 Botolph Street, Norwich where she later taught the Sunday School and spoke of an increasing interest of volunteering as a missionary in Africa.

The following year she began attending the Norwich Municipal Secondary Girls School where she received a good education and in 1919 she followed her dreams and applied to the North Africa Mission who appointed her jointly with the Mildmay Mission to the Jews. Elsie spoke of the true love shown by Jewish families. During the next decade Elsie worked in Algeria and Nabeul, Tunisia. She was described as a quiet, gracious compassionate woman who was deeply motivated by her calling.

By the 1930s Elsie had made her way to Europe where she offered spiritual guidance to Jewish refugees. By 1934 she had moved to Paris to continue her work and it was whilst in this occupation that she met a Jew named Leon Buchholz who begged her to travel to Vienna to collect his one-year-old daughter Ruth and bring her back to him in Paris. Days before the war began without a second's thought for her own safety Elsie completed the rescue whilst the Germans under Hitler began to rise up and take occupation of surrounding countries.

On 14th June 1940 Germany took Paris and Elsie, deciding to stay with her beloved adopted people, was incarcerated in a German prison camp at Vittel. The camp held foreign nationals including Jews with foreign passports (mostly obtained on the black market). These vital documents bought the bearer protection and most of all time, however limited. Vittel was not like most of the prison camps as it was located in requisitioned hotels. Commanded by Captain Otto Landhauser the 3,000 strong population were held at the spa resort located in the Vosges mountains near the German border. It was described as one of the most hospitable camps.

Elsie was now in her fifties and was chosen to work in the commandant's office as an archivist, where she took the risk of changing the Jewish internees' personal details, saving them from the Germans' goal of Endlösung der Judenfrage, translated as the final solution to the Jewish question. This was effectively the murder of all Jews in what became known as the Holocaust where 90% of Polish Jews and two thirds of Europe's entire Jewish population were sent to concentration camps to either work or die, mostly both.

In 1944 it became clear to Elsie that the Jewish people inside the camp were destined to be collected up and sent via a one-way train ticket to Auschwitz. With this realisation Elsie made her most dangerous move.

After meeting with a fellow internee, a young Polish machine-gunner named Sashe Krawech, she decided to protect him from the imminent train journey and to hide him in her bathroom for more than five months. Krawech had managed to survive the Warsaw Ghetto because he was a South African national. Elsie's decisive action saved the young man, ensuring he missed the repeated journeys to the camps.

Krawech gave a refreshing opinion of Elsie which makes her come to life. He reported that during the months he spent alongside Elsie, he found her so annoying he almost gave himself up to the Gestapo. Imagine being stuck in a tiny room with a 50-year-old unmarried missionary driven by her faith to convert those she encountered!! This wonderful real-life experience shows just how devoted Elsie was to her faith.

With the risk of the discovery of her hidden friend Elsie managed to survive until the Germans abandoned the camp on 12th September 1944. By that date over three hundred Jewish people interred at Vittel had not survived the war. However due to her brave action Krawech did manage to escape her bathroom untouched!

However, Elsie did manage one more heroic act. Before the camp prisoners were released, she managed to hide all the camp records and papers, destroying those which put others in immediate danger.

After her release Elsie stayed on until 1944 where she assisted with the repatriation of two hundred Jewish people.

Directly after the war she travelled to Lisbon and later to Africa where she continued her mission, returning to England in 1960.

Shortly afterwards, Elsie emigrated to America, arriving in New York on 30th July 1963. She settled close to her brother in Miami-Dade County in Florida where she worked as a nanny to several young children. It was whilst here that she fell and broke her hip. She was taken to Coral Gables Hospital where she peacefully passed away a week later. Her ashes were scattered over Biscayne Bay on the Atlantic Coast.

The baby, Ruth Bucholz, survived the war, later moving to the UK and marrying an Englishman. It was whilst searching for family history that her son, London barrister Professor Philippe Sands QC, found a yellowing note in a suitcase belonging to his mother. The note contained Elsie's address. It was this discovery that put a face to the mystery saviour who had rescued her from Austria.

The note read 'Menuka,' Bell Road, Norwich, Angleterre and Sands has since carried out a public search for the elusive address.

Due to a campaign run by Professor Sands, Elsie is one of twenty-one British people honoured as Righteous Among the Nations by Yad Vashem, the World Holocaust Remembrance Center in Jerusalem (Israel's official memorial to the victims of the holocaust) for heroism during the holocaust.

Sands commented that Elsie never expected acclaim for what she did but remembering her example may inspire the next generation.

Elsie never spoke to a soul about her actions during the war. It's only now after her death that her story can finally be told.

7. THE WOMEN'S TIMBER CORPS

It's Monday, 19th May 1942

A girl in her late teenage years stands with another upon the platform of the bustling station of her local town. The girls' hair is pinned up in matching victory rolls and shines with the vitality of youth. Each holds a small brown leather case containing the bare necessities for the summer season. Their excitement at their first trip away from home is etched in their faces along with the wide-eyed expression of uncertainty about leaving their parents' care.

As they board the train and select their seats, they accept an offer to assist them with their luggage into the rails above. Within thirty minutes the sooty engine puffs into Bury station where two burly soldiers lead them onto an awaiting truck.

After a short ride the girls look in awe at the barbed wire topped gates which open into a space filled with hastily constructed Nissen huts. Here they will put their training to use, here they will contribute, yet here their work will go on unnoticed and unappreciated to this very day.

The Women's Timber Corps came into being in April 1942 after Scandinavian countries under occupation could no longer export wood to England. Culford Camp became home to hundreds of young women known as Lumber Jills.

The WTC remain virtually unknown next to their counterparts in the Women's Land Army or Land Girls yet aside from the green beret these women's corps both contributed much towards the war effort.

Timber was needed for everything from building planes, making charcoal for explosives right down to providing wooden crosses to sit upon our heroes' final resting place.

After two weeks spent training the women were sent off to recognise, measure and fell trees in the woods. Working alongside men (who were the last to be conscripted), in 1942 alone these women saved 50 tons of shipping space per year.

The days began at 5.30 a.m. and ended at 3.30 p.m., ten hours of back-breaking work using manual saws then loading logs onto the waiting trucks. After the exhausting day came the option of venturing into Bury St Edmunds or staying to swap stories and sing round the camp's hearth.

These women faced constant prejudice from the men who expressed their disdain for these girls taking over their fellow working men's jobs but all held their heads high and wielded their 14lb axes like any man who had worked the forests before them.

The girls worked in all weathers risking serious injury yet gaining strong limbs and calloused hands. The lucky ones living close to home could have a bath each weekend but those from afar made do with a bucket and sponge!

Over 8,700 women worked as Lumber Jills yet received no recognition as a civilian service, and no assistance into post war placements.

These women, forgotten on the home front, were finally recognised in 2007 when a life size bronze statue of a Lumber Jill was unveiled in Queen Elizabeth Forest Park near Aberfoyle in Scotland dedicated to the Women's Timber Corps.

CHAPTER THREE

SOLDIERS'
STORIES

1. PRIVATE JOSEPH BONNEY

It's Tuesday, 1st June 1824

An ageing man, hair speckled with grey strands, stands tall in the colourful, sweet-scented garden of his lodging-house, located in the town of Sudbury, Suffolk. As he lingers, hands clasped behind his back, he is joined by another. The two men stroll past the rows of vegetables where they pause, the conversation turning to the size of this year's radish crop. Bending at the knees his neighbour reaches downwards as he gently eases the vegetable from the ground.

In one short swift lunge our man pulls a blade from inside his pantaloons. Glinting from the light of the sun the knife plunges between the crouching man's ribs. Now collapsed upon the lush green grass his white high-collared shirt rapidly turns red with loss of blood.

Mustering all his strength the victim calls out "Murder" and several persons come rushing to his aid. The attacker, dripping in his target's blood, calmly ambles through the garden gate and onto the bustling street, where soon he is apprehended and questioned as to his motive. In a calm and unperturbed manner, he replies "That deed ought to have been done eight months before".

Charged with intent to murder, our man awaits the summer assizes in the County Gaol located at Bury St Edmunds.

Joseph Bonney was born in the summer of 1776 to parents John and Hannah. Little is known of his early life but it is known he worked hard as a wool comber in Sudbury's dominant industry of the time.

On 16th July 1799 Joseph enlisted into the 17th Battalion of the Leicestershire Regiment of Foot. It is unknown whether Joseph had been enticed to accept the king's shilling or if he volunteered for a lifetime's dedication to the forces. From 1793 the British Army consisted of a small force of just 40,000 men. However, a push in recruitment saw numbers swell to 250,000 men, 50,000 of whom were Greek and German volunteers.

Life as a British soldier was challenging and tough but Joseph and his battalion received extensive training before being expected to join their comrades on the battlefield. Conditions were poor and the force was well known for its strict rules and its habit of handing out severe punishments for minor offences.

Joseph was described as 5ft 6ins with light hair, hazel eyes and with a fair complexion.

The 17th Battalion would have been dressed in the iconic British red coat and would have been provided with a flintlock musket more commonly known as "Brown Bess".

Each soldier would have received around 8d per day including money for beer.

The British Army was proud of its men with the Duke of Wellington being quoted as saying how they converted "the scum of the earth" into fine fellows.

From 17th Dec 1804 to 27th May 1823 Joseph and his battalion served in India where alongside the Honourable East India Company (who ruled India by proxy for the British Government) they began laying the foundation of the great Indian Empire.

Joseph saw active service in the battle of Sutlej in 1808 and in the Anglo-Nepalese war of 1814-16.

After grappling with the steep mountain paths and dense jungle the exhausted troops fought the battle of Jaithak. With a shortage of ammunition and dwindling numbers the British Army suffered the loss of three hundred dead and severely wounded troops.

As a result, "by mid-February, of the four British commanders in charge Gillespie was dead, Marley had deserted, Wood was harassed into inactivity, and Martindell was practically incapacitated by over-cautiousness."

In 1817 Joseph served during the relief of Nagpore after which the regiment was awarded its famous Tiger Badge celebrating its invaluable service and the exemplary conduct, marked courage and endurance shown by all members of the regiment.

On 3rd April 1823 Joseph was discharged in consequence of a long service consisting of twenty-four years and six months. His conduct was recorded in his discharge as "very sufficient". After a lifetime's service he was pensioned off, receiving a payment of 1s 6d a day.

However, Joseph had great difficulty in settling into civilian life. Even prior to his discharge he began to show a severe change in personality and was fined for assaulting the Constable of Sudbury (deliberately impossible to pay) and jailed for threatening the landlord of the Bull Inn.

In the spring of 1824 Joseph declined further into a haze of bizarre behaviour, challenging several persons in the town. This pattern of unsettling events culminated in the attack on 1st June where Joseph plunged a knife four inches deep into the chest of a local tailor, John Fordham.

During his appearance at the summer assizes in August 1824 Joseph stared keenly at the women sitting on the bench. Pale faced with sunken eyes he presented a wildness of expression highlighted by his projecting brow. It was stated in his defence that after his return from active service he had frequently exhibited symptoms of insanity which had arisen from being at times indisposed from the effects of the wounds he had received during his career.

His landlady at the time of the attack described his odd behaviour, such as dragging his bed around his room and sitting naked upon the stairs all night to "keep out the rogues".

John Orridge, keeper of the Bury St Edmunds gaol, swore that since Joseph had been under his care his conduct had been very strange, leaving no doubt that he was insane. At one point he had to be restrained after attacking another prisoner because of music. He often complained to the guards that men were entering his cell at night playing musical instruments and the rationale behind his attack on Mr. Fordham had been about this.

Joseph remained silent once he was asked for his plea and after a break, he returned the plea of "Not Guilty".

The jury after some discussion came to the conclusion that Joseph was to be acquitted on the grounds of insanity. It was suggested he should be confined and kept apart from other men in the goal.

In December 1824 it was suggested that he should be removed from the gaol to the lunatic asylum in Norwich. After their refusal to accommodate him, Joseph was sent to the asylum at Plaistow, Essex where he remained until a warrant signed by Robert Peel ordered his removal from his current residence to the Suffolk Asylum at Woodbridge.

On the morning of 24th June 1842, it is reported Joseph Bonney had passed away from a disease of the lungs.

During my research into Joseph's life, I felt saddened by his plight, thankfully in these modern times it's well-known how difficult it is for Army personnel to adjust into civilian life after such a long time spent in the routines of soldiering overseas. If Joseph had been alive today it would have been suggested that he was in fact suffering from the effects of Post-Traumatic Stress Disorder (PTSD) which presented itself soon after he was discharged. I wonder how his behaviour would be handled today and how the outcome could with the right help and medication have been so very different.

2. CAPTAIN CECIL TIDSWELL

It's Monday, 16th October 1916 - 2.25 p.m.

A pilot flying ahead of a formation leads eight other BE12 aircrafts above the infamous Somme. A successful mission completed, the group swerve and turn towards home. The sky, barely containing even one cloud, ensures a good view of the path ahead. As he banks to the left, he spies a large formation of aircraft headed into his chosen path. The wind rushing past his head fills his ears with a deafening hurricane, leaving little chance of hearing the roar of the faster enemy. As the guns begin to roar the aircraft dance in the sky, each trying to get in line to destroy, each praying to be the first. As the pilot begins to bring his craft lower in the sky an Albatross positions itself to his rear, quickly gaining on his craft. As he begins to climb up, he reaches 8,000 ft, trying to shake his tail. His goggles mist, reacting with the sweat upon his brow. With all attention focussed on the enemy behind his flimsy craft his group begin to fire. As an enemy attaches to his tail he swerves, using the brilliant glare of the hot sun to blind his foe. Despite his efforts nine hundred rounds pepper his plane leaving holes in both metal and muscle. He says a silent prayer as he cascades towards the ground spinning round and round till an impact ends his final mission. Pieces fly with an explosion of debris, filling the neatly ploughed field with twisted steel. The famous Red Baron Lieutenant Manfred Von Richthofen returns on a macabre visit. He cuts the serial number out of the fabric of the fuselage, another trophy to add to the collection of death which he takes such pride in.

Cecil Robert Tidswell was born on 22nd November 1880 at Creeting St Mary and baptised on 6th January the following year in Creeting's parish church up on the hill. His parents were Richard Henry 1848-1928, a barrister of law, and Helen Maude née Brooke 1854-1941. The Tidswells were lucky enough to own Bosmere Hall (at this time within the borders of the Creetings) and all the land associated with the estate and raised eight children there, one boy, Cecil, and seven girls.

Cecil was educated at Harrow from 1894-1898. I found him listed after that as a successful candidate at the competitive examination held in June, 1898 for cadets at the Royal Military College at Sandhurst, where he was selected for the Calvary. In 1899 the second Boer war broke out in South Africa; in 1901 he was transferred to the 7th Battalion Kings Royal Rifle Corps and in the same year he also attended The School of Musketry in Hythe St Leonard in Kent, listed as an officer. In the August he transferred to the Royal Dragoons where he had several family connections and served with that regiment in Durban, South Africa during the Second Boer War. The Royal or 1st Dragoons were dressed in scarlet uniforms with blue facings and a black plume.

In the November of 1900 his regiment was sent to relieve Ladysmith taking part in the battles of Spion Kop and the Tugela Heights. They achieved great success in January 1900 where they managed to ambush a column of over two hundred Boers near Acton Homes and succeeded in trapping forty of the enemy. During 1901, the regiment were responsible for guarding the Buffalo River and protecting the Transvaal. As a direct result of experiences gained during this expedition the rifle superseded the sword in the importance of weaponry during times of conflict. For his service in Africa Cecil earned both the Queen's and the King's South Africa Medals and five clasps.

Between 1903 and 1907 the Royal Dragoons were sent to serve in India beginning in Lucknow then in Secunderabad and Muttia in Agra.

Apart from keeping the Indian locals under English control the regiment were responsible for giving a firm military response to frequent terrorist attacks on the British.

While serving in the Army the soldiers enjoyed and were encouraged in the practice of pig sticking, or boar hunting. The sport was encouraged by the military as it was good calvary training, due to the degree of horsemanship required to catch the cunning and ferocious wild boar. The men also played polo and enjoyed shooting. That is not to say they did not work hard. Their days began at 6.30 a.m. sharp and training took up the entire morning, finishing at lunch.

An amusing story I found during my research included the regiment sergeant betting one of his men that if he could ride a particularly wild and stubborn horse without being thrown off, he would be awarded a month's leave. The soldier accepted the challenge. Unfortunately for the sergeant the dragoon did manage to ride the horse and stayed mounted giving the boss little choice but to make good on his promise and allow the dragoon his leave!

3. SKIPPER THOMAS CRISP

It's Wednesday, 15th August 1917 - 2.45 p.m.

A man stands proudly over his haul trying to estimate the morning catch. After the nets are in and the fish made ready, they begin to sweep the ocean looking for the enemy. His heart quickens as he spots something on the horizon. He shouts clearly, and the men aboard drag the heavy tarpaulin from the three-pounder gun. Almost at once there comes the deafening sound of shellfire from the German submarine as three shells narrowly miss the ship. The noise is unimaginable as her guns fire and they sail closer within range. Confident that they will outgun them, he stands clearly on the bow almost tempting the enemy to wound him. The fourth shell hits, tearing flesh from bone and smashing through the bow. He falls to the floor as his legs splinter into a hundred pieces. In spite of his severe injuries, he calls his son to his side and gives his final orders and demands "Tom I'm done, throw me overboard".

Thomas Crisp was born on 28th April 1876 to William and Mary Ann. One of ten children, life was comfortable and there was always good food on the table. His father owned a prominent ship building yard; therefore, all his children were given the best education money could buy. However, Thomas did not settle well into his schooling, thinking he would much rather be amongst the hustle and bustle of the quayside. As soon as he was able, he left school and joined a fishing trawler as a herring fisherman. He was born for it, took to it like a duck to water! He quickly tired of the limitations of his new career, finding a position on the SS Mobile, an Atlantic steamship. Within no time Thomas was promoted to quartermaster. Both working and playing hard (as young boys do) he met and fell hopelessly in love with a beautiful girl and on 2nd June 1895 Harriet Elizabeth Alp accepted his hand in marriage.

In 1897, their first-born entered the world. A little girl named Harriet. She was followed in 1899 by Thomas junior. Thinking his family complete, Thomas senior continued with his career and in 1902, he landed a dream job with Chambers, the biggest boat-owning family in Lowestoft. For thirteen happy years he sailed upon the ketch LT956 George Borrow, becoming the most popular fishing captain in town.

In 1910, Thomas and Harriet were surprised by the arrival of another child who they named Charles and in 1913 Thomas saw his proudest moment to date when his son Thomas junior joined him on the George Borrow. A year passed and after fishing for days in the North Sea the crew came home to hear that Britain was officially at war with Germany and enemy submarines were expected at port any moment. Thomas was too old for general service and was working within a vital position so continued his work, keeping his eyes open for the expected submarines. By September so many ships had been sunk that it became the norm to find bodies of the drowned servicemen, swollen, cold, entangled in the nets.

In 1915 Thomas junior signed up and joined the Royal Navy. The expected submarines arrived, sinking fishing boats to reduce food availability to the Brits. In August Thomas's beloved George Borrow was sunk. When the Navy came scouting for experienced fishermen he, without a second's thought signed up to serve his country. The Navy secretly armed small fishing boats to protect the vessels from attack. Arranging for Thomas junior to serve by his side, he was conscripted to a Q ship, the HM armed smack I'll Try (originally registered as the G&E).

He was offered a promotion and a transfer to an ocean-going Q ship but he was forced to decline as his wife had fallen terminally ill. By June, that year she had passed away leaving her family devastated by the loss.

In January, 1917, the smack and her crew experienced their first confrontation with the enemy. With the assistance of a larger boat, the Boy Alfred, two German submarines were hit and reported as probably sunk, earning both skippers the Distinguished Service Cross (DSC). In order to maintain cover after this incident, the I'll Try was re-named the Nelson and the Boy Alfred became the Ethel and Millie.

It's Wednesday, 15th August 1917

Thomas, with critical injuries, orders all confidential papers to be thrown overboard. His son is bent over, ear to his beloved father's lips, relaying his orders.

One of their four carrier pigeons was sent bearing the message. 'Nelson being attacked by submarine, Skipper killed, Jim Howe Bank assistance at once' As the crew floated the lifeboat, the Nelson took on more and more water, crew members despite his protests attempted to save Thomas but sadly minutes later he passed away cradled in his son's arms. Nine unwounded crew members abandoned ship as the Ethel and Millie arrived to help but Nelson's crew refused to board, fearing their weight could sink her. Instead, she sailed straight towards the sub under lethal fire. She was soon damaged and took on water. The crew were taken on board the submarine as prisoner but were never seen or heard of again.

Nelson's survivors drifted for two days before rescue. The pigeon had reached the authorities. Afterwards, at the court of enquiry, Nelson's crew were praised and Thomas Crisp was awarded the Victoria Cross. After prime minister David Lloyd George's speech in the House of Commons, Thomas became a national hero with his face in every newspaper. He is memorialised on his wife's gravestone at Lowestoft cemetery and also commemorated on the Chatham Naval Memorial.

One hundred years after his death, a stone was laid at the Naval Memorial in Belle Vue Park, Lowestoft to ensure that younger generations remember him. This story was written in the hope that we go on to remember Thomas and be thankful for his service.

None of the Ethel and Millie's crew were civilians. Two were RN sailors: Able Seamen Edwin Barrett and Alfred Preece. The others were members of the RNR: Skipper Charles Manning, 2nd Hand Spencer Gibson and Deck Hands John Lewis, Arthur Soames and Hugh Thompson. May they rest in peace.

4. PRIVATE SAMUEL HARVEY VC

It's Friday, 29th September 1915

A soldier hunches down in the mud, trembling hands covering his ears, desperately trying to drown out the sound of gunfire and shells exploding just yards away. The endless heavy rain soaks his hair, droplets running down into his smock and sending violent chills down his back. He catches a breath. Ahead, comrades throw more pineapple-shaped bombs, each time straining to hurl the grenade closer to them. The enemy. A deep, strained voice shouts for volunteers. He steps closer, tilting his head to hear the commanding officer speak. The bombs are scarce; someone must visit the supply dump to keep the Germans at bay. Clearing his dry throat, he speaks up, claiming the task as his own. Within minutes the soldier is moving through pools of fetid water, earth clumping to boots with every step. Bodies lie in the path, some in the stillness of death, others writhing and screaming in burning agony. Men huddled in groups try desperately to stop the thick fresh blood oozing through their fingers. He moves onwards taking lefts and rights and becoming numb to the suffering he passes. Finally, he arrives. With a clear head, a voice inside tells him over and over, "too slow, too slow." Heaving the wooden crate into his arms he sets off again, plotting a quicker route. Stumbling onto the open ground he pauses and fills his lungs with cold damp air. He sprints onwards, feeling the guns moving, adjusting their aim. The bullets whizz by as he reaches his goal. Over and over, he retraces his path. The sun, rising, battles the rain. Upon reaching open ground, a searing, tearing pain explodes through his skull. He has made his final journey that day.

Samuel Harvey was born in 1881, along with his twin sister Mahala, at 3 Annersley Place, Bulwell, near Basford, in Nottinghamshire. He was one of nine children and his Suffolk-born parents William, a farm labourer and Mary Ann née Calver, a charwoman, worked hard to support their large family. A year later they moved back to Suffolk, to Ipswich. Samuel, fondly nicknamed Monkey for his cheeky humour, attended the Argyle Street School where he received a good education, but he never really settled.

In 1897, he was brought before Ipswich Police Court for several counts of stealing and sent to Warwickshire Reformatory school for three years. After his release he lived at 36 Bell Street, Ipswich working as a labourer for his master William Grimwood. By February 1903 he had joined the army in the 3rd Battalion of the Suffolk regiment, where he is described as 5ft 3ins with a pale complexion, brown hair and blue eyes, "a handsome young man". Samuel, though, was never far from trouble. He was arrested for disturbing the peace and on more counts of stealing in July then, in the November, he is charged with an assault of a police officer after knocking the constable down and violently kicking him whilst on the ground. For that he received six weeks' hard labour in prison. At this point he is labelled by his superiors as bearing a bad character. After many episodes of bad behaviour, he was dishonourably discharged but that would not stop Samuel.

By 1905, he'd re-joined the army in the York and Lancaster Regiment. He quickly earned a promotion to Lance Corporal and was stationed in India for seven years before being transferred to the reserve.

In 1914, after the outbreak of WWI, Samuel was recalled to the army and served in the British Expeditionary Force until the events of 29th September. In "Big Willie Trench" at the battle of Loos he earns the Victoria Cross for his bravery. Delivering 350 Mills bombs to the front whilst risking life and limb, stopping the advancing Germans in their tracks. After being shot in the head he was wounded a further three times, resulting in him walking with a limp from then on. In October 1916 he was transferred to the 3rd Battalion of the Northumberland Fusiliers and whilst on leave in 1917, he received his Victoria Cross. It is said that King George V personally pinned on the award whilst Samuel winked at Queen Mary and joked "Mine's a pint!" In May 1918, he was honourably discharged.

Like many others, Samuel found it hard to get work after the war due to his injuries, earning his wage by digging people's gardens. For a short time, he was an ostler at the Great White Hotel, Ipswich, taking care of the horses, but life never seemed to go well for him and he lived for a number of years in a wooden hut in Wolves Wood, Hadleigh and in the Salvation Army hostel in Fore Street, Ipswich. During this time, he lost his Victoria Cross. One story says he traded it for a pint, another that he lost it in the woods whilst sleeping rough.

In 1944 and aged sixty-four, he married Georgina Brown, five years his senior, at St Peter's Church in Ipswich but it was rumoured that the match was unhappy and he was regularly seen sleeping off a boozy night on the steps of Ipswich Town Hall. Within a few short years Georgina died from complications of diabetes. Samuel's own health continued to decline and after injuring his hip he attended the 1956 Victoria Cross Centenary celebrations in London's Hyde Park sitting in a wheelchair.

Sadly, after sixteen months at Stow Lodge Hospital, Stowmarket (the much-feared former workhouse), on 23rd September 1960 he passed away from myocardial degeneration and senility. Penniless and alone.

He was buried in an unmarked communal grave in Old Ipswich Cemetery on the 27th, its location being Plot X, Division 21, Grave 3.

After his death his miniature medals were found kept under his pillow (showing I believe his pride in his heroism). Samuel had earned the Victoria Cross, the 1914 star with Mons clasp, the British War medal and the George V and Elizabeth II coronation medals during his time at war. He was also made Knight, Legion d'Honneur 5th Class (France) and awarded the Cross of St George (4th Class) (Russia).

In 2000, forty years after his death, a ceremony was held and a memorial headstone erected to the lone call of a Salvation Army bugler.

In 2013, a campaign led by a group from Park View Care Home saw to renovating his memorial, planting a commemorative tree and placing a stone slab in the entrance to Christchurch Park, Ipswich.

5. CORPORAL ALBERT THOMAS ABRAHAM

It's Sunday, 23rd August 1914 - 9.00 a.m.

The battle of Mons had begun in earnest. The 3rd Battalion of the Coldstream Guards were eager to start the job they had been trained for, readied for the first battle between the British and German forces of the First World War. The guns were placed on high ground and the bombardment developed when the German Infantry advanced in close formations. However, losing heavily, the battalion retreated, leaving heavy casualties.

On 31st August, just as the battalion were about to retire for the night, a horse and cart came into sight in the distance. Thinking it contained refugees, the men were relaxed. Instead, the cart contained a machine-gun that opened fire at close range. Miraculously there were no casualties or even much damage at all. Under intensive fire the battalion withdrew to their earlier position in the forest. The colonel at once realised he had a very long line to defend in thick woodlands. By 11.00 a.m. they were under a vicious attack with all battalions heavily engaged. The Germans found the gaps in the defence and penetrated the lines and the Coldstream Guards retreated slowly, fighting in isolated battles. After a time, the enemy withdrew and at 2.00 p.m. the British retired.

On 1st September the brigade encountered fierce opposition, losing heavily with casualties numbering some three hundred. The 3rd Battalion losses were eight killed, twenty wounded and eight missing, one being Albert Abraham who was shot through the lung by a rifle and was cut off with a small number of comrades. Captain Sinclair of the (Royal) Army Medical Corps, their medical officer, was sent back with the medical supplies to assist the injured. However, he was captured and lacking any further supplies the wounded had no chance of receiving medical aid. Picked up by the enemy, they were interred in camps across Germany.

Albert Thomas Abraham was born in the parish of St John's, Bury St Edmunds in 1883 to Thomas and Eliza Frost who lived at 107 Madras Terrace. In 1891 he is listed in the census as living at 109 Northgate Road, his father being an engine driver. He was a fireman by trade but not finding enough excitement in that role he joined the army in 1902. Private 4780 of the 3rd Battalion of the Coldstream Guards is described as 5ft 10ins tall, weighing 138 lbs with a fair complexion and light brown hair. He seemed to have a period of unrest, as in 1907 he was marked as "wilfully absenting himself from parade when employed as instructor to recruits". Five days later he escaped barracks whilst being a prisoner at large under medical treatment. He was severely reprimanded but that did not stop him from an attempt at obtaining leave in an improper manner in 1911. Beforehand he had been promoted to Corporal, a promotion he was lucky enough not to have lost.

In August 1914 Abraham was sent with the British Expeditionary Force to France where he was shot in the chest and captured. As a prisoner of war, he was kept in Germany and later in Holland. He was released once the war ended and was discharged as physically unfit. He died in Greenwich in 1920 from injuries obtained in battle.

6. SERGEANT WILLIAM FINCH

It's Sunday, 17th September 1916

A solitary survivor wearing military uniform with mask thrown over his shoulder is struggling, wading through the deep mud of no man's land, trying desperately to reach the relative safety of the trench ahead. Finally releasing his left leg, he takes another step and sinks up to his knees. He is stuck. He tilts his head, sniffs the air, it's coming, the tell-tale odour of pineapple and peppers. Quickly he swings his mask and pulls it over his face. The pale green fog rolls in completely obscuring the soldier. Later, his reunited battalion went over the top, all playing mouth organs as they fought the Germans close by.

William George Finch was born in June 1884 to Zepho and Eliza née Killington. The couple had married hastily in the April in Depwade, Norfolk with Zepho doing the manly thing and making an honest woman out of Eliza, who was seven months pregnant. William was educated from 1888 at Loddon in the school on Church Plain where he learnt to read and write and play his beloved football. Choosing a career as a master builder, he married Olive Barlow in 1901. They were happy raising four children together in the village of Loddon in Norfolk.

Come 1914, war broke out and at the age of thirty-three William signed up and requested to join the Middlesex Regiment, 17th (Service) Football Battalion.

(Of course, as soon as you mention football together with the war you instantly think of the truce on Christmas day where Germans and English troops played a game, sharing cigarettes and proudly showing off photographs of loved ones. I instantly thought this regiment was a great idea, bringing people together with a passion for the game and curious to find more information I began to research William even more closely.)

Originally the 17th was set up as a "Pals battalion" by William Joyson-Hicks in Fulham Town Hall, London. Hicks personally encouraged 120 professional players and 500 fans to form the Football Battalion of the Middlesex Regiment. He imagined that the public, desperate for entertainment and normality, would support his plans. Unfortunately, the media portrayed the battalion in a negative light and the general public followed.

By 1916, the battalion were fully trained and the troop embarked for France. Between 14th and 17th July 1916, they marched to a stronghold named Delville Wood, located near Longueval in dense forest with trees twisting and turning together into a thick tangle of branches. There they fought in the first engagement of the Battle of the Somme followed closely by the Battle of Bazentin Ridge. For the rest of the summer, they fought for control of the wood whilst enduring the wet weather and thick mud. By the end of the month, German fatalities totalled 160,000 men and the Anglo-French had lost 200,000.

Next, they fought in the battle at Guillemont on 8th August 1916. The battalion lost so many men that the Middlesex needed a draft of 716 more to bring it back up to strength.

On 13th November 1916, the Middlesex attacked the Redan Ridge, near Serre, in the Battle of the Ancre. After weeks of heavy rain, some men sank up to their waists in the mud and a heavy fog hung over the battlefield, limiting visibility to thirty yards. William was finally sent home, where he spent some time in the Norwich and Norfolk hospital as his lungs were weak from the gas attacks. From June, 1917, William was to serve on the home front with the 601st Home Service Employment Company of the Labour Corps where he was involved in salvage operations.

In February, 1919, William was appointed sergeant and he requested to join the Royal Defence Corps, a regiment for soldiers who were too old or medically unfit for front line service. There his battalion were responsible for guarding ports and bridges. By April 1918, there were 27,000 men in the RDC, 14,000 of them working as guards in the prisoners of war encampments.

After bringing up his family and living a quiet country life William died in October 1948 in Loddon, Norfolk.

7. PRIVATE FREDERICK JAMES OVERTON

It's September 1916

A man stands upright in the pouring rain, his uniform heavy and sodden. Lightning flashes across the sky, illuminating his comrades. Men, rifles ready, staring into the dark, waiting.

Frederick James Overton was born in April 1894, to James and Emma Overton in Back lane, Needham Market, where he attended the local school. Later he attended the Duke of York Royal Military School and the Queen Victoria School.

After working as a labourer in an explosives factory, on 13th August 1914 Frederick joined the Suffolk Regiment, part of the British Expeditionary Force who were among the first to be sent to France. Private 551632 is described as being 5ft 7ins tall and weighing 128 lbs with a fresh complexion, light brown hair and hazel eyes. He had a tattoo on his right forearm of two crossed flags. He was of good character, honest and a hard worker.

The battalion's first posting was at the Mons-Condé Canal where they attempted to hold the line from the enemy, but after heavy losses they were forced to begin a two-week retreat. However, Frederick was not among the men. He wasn't in France at all. The documents show that he never even left England.

On 4th May 1916, Frederick James Overton was tried by court martial at Bury St Edmonds, for desertion, from 14th August 1914, the day after he enlisted. He was apprehended by a local civil power on 9th April 1916 after nearly two years on the run. In court he was convicted and sentenced to serve three years in His Majesty's Royal Army, then sent to the 15th Infantry Base Depot in Calais to wait for his posting.

It's Tuesday, 12th September 1916

The relentless rain has turned the ground to mud, the type of mud that sticks in heavy clumps to his boots. Frederick is finally in France, ready to serve his country.

Frederick was transferred from the Suffolks to the 1st Battalion of the Bedfordshire Regiment who were described as brave and determined, and known for singing and laughing even under the most extreme conditions. Through September and November 1916, the 1st Battalion were involved in the heavy fighting at the Battle of the Somme where the British lost 450,000 men.

April 1917 saw the Battle of Arras where the Bedfords were responsible for holding a boundary close to a railway track. In the skirmishes Frederick was wounded after being shot in his left thigh. He was first taken to the a casualty clearing station and then put onto an ambulance train for a stationary hospital followed by two convalescent depots at Boulogne and Écault. He was sent to a base depot for a couple of weeks and had recovered enough to re-join his battalion on the 25th June.

Three days later he received another gunshot wound, this time in his right leg! He was taken to a field ambulance first, then a casualty clearing station and finally to a Red Cross Hospital.

On the 31st July 1917 he re-joined his battalion, who were en route to relieve the Devonshire Regiment in the reserve trenches. Later that year the whole battalion were on working parties when unluckily Frederick was involved in an accident, not his fault, ending in a fractured tibia. This time he was treated first at a casualty clearing station and then at a Red Cross Hospital, then he was taken on an ambulance train to a general hospital and Her Majesty's Hospital Ship Grandtully Castle brought him home to England.

On the 12th April 1918 Frederick was transferred to the Labour Corps, the 579th Home Service Employment Company in the Eastern region. Soldiers here, too old or unfit for service on the front line, were involved in the day to day running of the depot. 400,000 men served in these battalions, divided into employment companies across the country.

Frederick was discharged as medically unfit for service in June 1918, not long before the end of the war after serving over two years of his sentence. He received the British War and the Victory Medal.

In 1925, Rose Ansell married Frederick in the Gipping district. They went on to have a happy family and grew old together.

He passed away in 1980 after a remarkable life.

He is buried at St John the Baptist Cemetery in Barrett's Lane, Needham Market.

CHAPTER FOUR

Famous Faces

1. THOMAS WOLSEY

It's Saturday, 23rd June 1520

A man stands at the altar, dressed in a magnificent cassock stitched out of the finest cloth of gold and stretching over his portly belly. That man, bearing the title of cardinal, surveys the scene with personal satisfaction. The chapel, one of many temporary constructions and imitating a solid chapel akin to those back over the Channel in England, is built from timber with stretched canvas painted to imitate bricks and the slate tiles on the timber roof. Underfoot the finest Turkish carpet covers the floor for the comfort of the kings in attendance. Through the large stained-glass windows, the sun is setting for the night and pitches rays of red and orange light, almost bringing the painted glass alive. From the canvas walls hang elegant tapestries, each depicting scenes from the sermons he recites directly from the Bible. God's words. Both French and English choirs are gathered together, taking it in turn to sing exquisite harmonies supporting the Mass about to be celebrated. Reciting the holy service was a personal honour, saying Mass in the presence of two magnificent kings seated serenely side by side, indicating that the cardinal's plans for peace are progressing nicely. As the chapel empties the crowd stares up at the crimson sky where they see a dragon, combining the salamander emblem of Francis I with Henry VIII's Welsh Tudor dragon. The kite has been constructed from timber hoops with cloth stretched over and is being pulled across the sky by a long rope attracted to a carriage. The spectators gasp in awe as the dragon's eyes blaze and through its mouth comes the sound of hissing (most probably achieved with the use of fireworks). The cardinal filling the frame of the tent's entrance smiles, his planning and hard work these months is going exactly how he wished. He says a short prayer in his head that this should be the end of all war between England and France.

Thomas Wolsey was born in 1473 to hardworking parents Robert Wolsey a butcher and Joan Daundy who was supporting the running of the household. Wolsey attended Ipswich School and Magdalen

College School, continuing to study theology at Magdalen College in Oxford. By March 1498 he was ordained as a priest to serve in Marlborough in Wiltshire. Choosing to remain in Oxford, however, Thomas was appointed Master of Magdalen College School but from 1500-1509 he answered his calling and became the rector of St Mary's Church in Limington, Somerset.

Attracting attention for his organized professional manner he was soon invited to become Chaplain to Henry Deane, the Archbishop of Canterbury and when looking for lodgings he was taken in by Sir Richard Nanfan, the deputy lieutenant of Calais, who selected Wolsey as executor of his estate. After Nanfan's death in 1507 Wolsey entered the service of Henry VII as royal chaplain. When Henry VIII succeeded his father in 1509, the young king worried little about Wolsey's poor origins, concentrating only on the success he had worked so hard for. Henry, after completing state business in Scotland moved Wolsey to the role of Almoner (an official distributor of alms) earning him a seat within the privy council. By 1515 Wolsey had climbed the ranks to become Lord Chancellor where he set about trying to destroy the reputations of other competing courtiers, even attempting to persuade the King to execute both Brandon and Mary Tudor for marrying in secret. Luckily for them the king did not accept his advice on this occasion. The nobles knew what Wolsey was attempting and one by one the court turned against him and his cunning plans which made him very unpopular.

Wolsey lived a non-canonical life, seeing for a decade a woman named Joan Larke from Yarmouth with whom he had two children, a daughter and a son. He was able to provide the best education for them and ensured that his son had the best tutor, Maurice Birchinshaw of St Paul's School, while his daughter was adopted by a John Cansey, maybe an alderman in Worcestershire, and sent to study in Shrewsbury Nunnery. Between 1514 and 1523 Wolsey collected title after title, arranging three peace treaties and beginning to build and renovate his homes. Not forgetting his roots, he founded a school in Ipswich. He was made Bishop of Durham and later accepted an appointment from Pope Leo X, making him a cardinal and allowing him a wide political influence. Later as Papal legate he organised one of the most magnificent celebrations in history.

He planned to end the war in France. After arranging for the king to sign the Treaty of London there began the lengthy process of outlawing war forever between Christian countries, starting by bringing both English and French kings together to share an eighteen-day festival full of entertainment and feasts.

With just two months to plan the whole of the proceedings Wolsey crossed the Channel, choosing common ground for an event that he wanted to be remembered in history as the "Field of the Cloth of Gold". In a pasture near Calais, France he set about building a temporary palace with towers, chapels, banqueting halls, kitchens and bed chambers fit for a King. Master craftsmen created a small village from timber and cloth. One such building (the only one with brick foundations) was constructed with both walls and roof entirely of golden cloth but just days before the arrival of the crowds it was swept away by gale force winds.

Once constructed, the small village made of timber and canvas was ready for the finishing touches to be added. Wolsey filled the spaces with fine carpets, embroidered wall hangings and countless huge glass windows. He added statues and courtyards boasting fountains flowing with red wine. This was to be a display of wealth shown to Henry's rival.

The first day of the event the two kings observed one another upon their horses from either side of the valley. Henry demanded that his followers, three thousand foot-soldiers and five hundred horsemen (not including all the lords, barons, knights and gentlemen) stand completely still on pain of death. He began to ride out to greet the French king. As they met Wolsey, squinting into the distance, saw them embrace, dismount from their horses and embrace again, both removing their hats then strolling arm in arm to a tent in order to begin their meeting. This became the most memorable festivals of all time, all organised and choreographed by Wolsey. Over the course of the festival the two kings enjoyed and competed in jousting, archery, masquerades and wrestling. Wolsey took pains not to set the two kings up against each other in direct competition but when Henry challenged Francis to a wrestling match, Francis agreed beating Henry in minutes. However, Henry soon recovered his pride after winning at archery, his long bow being far too heavy for the French king. After eighteen days of fun and excitement the two men exchanged gifts, Henry giving a collar of diamonds and Francis giving a highly expensive bracelet. They parted as friends with the two Kings returning home and Wolsey confident in the new friendly alliance.

The next task which Henry gave Wolsey was the beginning of his downfall. Henry was to send Wolsey to use his influence with the Pope to arrange a papal annulment of his marriage to Catherine of Aragon, making him free to marry Ann Boleyn. After attempting this impossible task and trying to follow his orders Wolsey failed, partly due to the Holy Roman Emperor, Charles V of Spain, being a cousin of Catherine's. Ann Boleyn despised Wolsey now even more and took great pleasure in whispering false accusations into King Henry's ear making him lose all confidence in Wolsey.

First Wolsey was stripped of all of his properties then of his titles. Still holding the archbishopric of York, he travelled there only to be arrested at Cawood Castle, his palace in York, and recalled to London to answer the charge of treason (a common accusation to rid Henry of troublesome priests). Upon reaching Leicester Abbey Wolsey became gravely ill with dysentery and died there on Tuesday 29th November. He is buried at the location marked with a stone in the Abbey Park. The lavish funeral he had planned would never happen and his ornate black sarcophagus was used to bury Lord Nelson within St Paul's Cathedral.

One would hope that Wolsey would have left one lasting treaty but after Charles VI attacked part of France, England yet again got dragged into the fight and by 1521 they were back at war, shattering the peace in Europe once more and with the festival and friendship quite forgotten.

2. AMBROSE ROOKWOOD

"Remember, remember the 5th of November - gunpowder, treason and plot. We see no reason why gunpowder treason should be ever be forgot."

Suffolk's little-known connection to the Gunpowder Plot.

It's Sunday, 5th November 1605 London - 10.00 p.m.

A man short in stature strides towards his finely saddled mount. Dressed extravagantly in a tight satin doublet and gold braided hose, he flings back his cape and leaps upon the horse. Wasting no time, he gallops away from London shivering in the cold air and shrinking from the torrential rain. By the time he reaches his gang, they having left earlier, he has covered thirty miles in just two hours.

Passing through the towns the gang numbers swell with the hope of a catholic uprising ahead. Soon they arrive at Holbeach House, near Dudley in Staffordshire, the home of their fellow extremist Stephen Lyttleton.

The hundred-strong gang begin to ready the house for an imminent siege, preparing the stolen weapons and laying out damp gunpowder before the fire with the hope that it will dry in time.

Once news of the failed plot had travelled and Catesby had advised those not willing to die to escape at once, just twelve men remained. Later that night and huddling around the hearth, the men all jump to attention as a stray spark ignites the explosives, causing burns to our man's face and blinding another.

By eleven o'clock the following morning the house is surrounded by two hundred armed men under orders from Richard Walsh, the Sheriff of Worcester.

With the offer to surrender ignored, the Sheriff's men begin the siege by setting fires around the house, aiming to flush out their targets. As the guilty hold firm, the Sheriff's posse load their muskets and open fire on the house, leaving musket holes on most of the interior walls.

Inside the courtyard our man desperately attacks the fire by beating the growing flames. As he raises his arms an agonising pain tears through his flesh. Violently twisting, he falls to the ground, grasping his right arm in an attempt to staunch the flow of the gushing blood.

Within minutes the house is stormed by the officers who begin the search for trophies, turning furniture up on end, ripping out drawers and tipping the contents to the ground. Whilst they search for loot the dying men, offered no medical assistance, breathe their last.

The battle once over leaves four men dead and two wounded whilst others escape.

The living pair are taken immediately by cart to be confined at Worcester Jail whilst they await their transport back to London.

Ambrose Rookwood was born in 1578 to a wealthy Catholic family with over three hundred years of rich ancestors before them. He was the eldest son of Robert and Dorothea who, so loyal to their faith, had been imprisoned and fined for recusancy (religious non-conformity). The family were known to the authorities as troublemakers due to another member, their cousin Edward, having spent ten years in prison for his faith. He had previously entertained Queen Elizabeth I at his home, Euston Hall, in Suffolk, which had made a considerable dent in the family's finances.

The Rookwood family owned a vast estate, and had chosen to reside at Stanningfield Hall, Bury St Edmunds, Suffolk for thirty years.

Rookwood and his siblings were educated by Jesuits and were among the first to be tutored at St Omer, France then later at Flanders.

Once grown Rookwood was described as "well built and handsome, if somewhat short" with a taste for extravagant fashion which confirmed his social standing. Whilst his siblings joined the church Rookwood, who had a natural way with horses, set up a fine stable at Coldham Hall, Norfolk where he bred the most sought-after mounts of the time.

In 1599, Rookwood married the wealthy Roman Catholic Elizabeth Tyrwhitt of Kettleby, Lincolnshire and sired two heathy young boys, thus continuing his line.

In 1600 he inherited his father's extensive estates, his wealth and titles attracting the attention of his close friend Robert Catesby.

In a bold move Rookwood commissioned a London cutler to produce a sword using a hilt and a Spanish blade engraved with the passion of Christ. With the intention to wear in public "a potentially dangerous statement of faith".

Disillusioned by unfulfilled promises by James I to show leniency towards Catholics, Catesby enlisted Rookwood into a plot to assassinate the King and other dignitaries and create an uprising where they would kidnap his nine-year-old daughter Princess Elizabeth and install her onto the throne as titular queen, meaning in name only.

Planned to coincide with the Opening of Parliament, the plan was delayed due to an outbreak of Plague.

One of the gang, Thomas Percy, had secured the basement below the House of Lords. Guy Fawkes, an expert in explosives, transported thirty-six barrels of gunpowder into the basement.

However, little did they know but Francis Tresham had sent a note to a Member of Parliament advising him not to attended the opening of Parliament. This letter was shown to the king who ordered a search and found Guy Fawkes there. Somewhat amusingly Fawkes convinced the leader of the king's party that he was merely a servant guarding the basement. Unfortunately for Fawkes, upon the second search he was once again discovered, this time with matches in his possession.

Once arrested, Fawkes refused to talk but, under the orders of the King, he was tortured until he admitted the plot and named his co-conspirators.

On discovery of Fawkes' arrest, Rookwood rushed to inform the others who at once fled to the Midlands, knowing that the king's men would soon be upon them. Rookwood was the last to leave. He caught up with his gang and together they all gathered at Holbeach Hall, Staffordshire.

The owners, the Lyttleton family, were trusted friends who were well known for their part in Catholic uprisings and in particular in the Earl of Essex's Uprising of 1601. Once preparations were complete, a member inquired what the group intended to do. Rookwood replied "We mean to die here". After the siege the survivors were taken from Worcester to London.

Imprisoned in the Tower of London, Rookwood scratched his name into the wall of his cell in the Martin Tower where it can still be seen to this day.

On 27th January 1606 the surviving conspirers were gathered in Westminster Hall. Rookwood pleaded guilty. He reported that he had dreams of bringing Catholicism back to England and explained that he had only joined the conspiracy due to his friendship with Catesby whom he loved "above any worldly man". Rookwood pleaded for mercy so as not to leave a "blemish and blot unto all ages" His plea ignored, Rookwood was found guilty of treason and sentenced to be hung, drawn and quartered.

On 31st January 1606 Rookwood was tied to a wattled hurdle and dragged by a horse through the crowds in the Strand. Passing his home, he called out to his wife Elizabeth "Pray for me" she replied "I will and be of good courage. Offer thy self wholly to God. I for my part do as freely restore thee to God as he gave thee to me". He then closed his eyes in prayer for the rest of the journey.

Once arrived the three surviving members of the gang climbed up towards the waiting noose, each at peace with their demise. However, in one final act of rebellion Fawkes suddenly leapt from the scaffold, hitting the stone slabs, at once breaking his neck and thus avoiding the noose.

Rookwood upon his turn addressed the crowd, asking for God to bless the King and Queen and beseeching God to make the King a Catholic. After the men were executed, they were each drawn and quartered in Old Palace Yard at Westminster. Their remains were sent to the four corners of England as a warning.

Interestingly, we do not hear of the rest of the gang's involvement, though there were thirteen of them, and only learn of Guy Fawkes and his contribution, even though he was not the leader and only played a small part in the plot.

3. HORATIO NELSON

It's Wednesday, 8th January 1806

At Whitehall Stairs a solemn flotilla of boats with the Royal Navy's finest on board has brought the deceased on a black barge from Greenwich. Resting in his coffin in the centre under a black velvet throw lies Nelson the hero, preserved in spirits of wine. Above sits a canopy topped with plumes of black feathers. The drums beat out a rhythm as the trumpets play. On board, lieutenants of the Royal Navy in full dress uniform with black waistcoats, breeches and stockings accompany the deceased.

The barge is rowed into place, one of four draped in black cloth and carrying the commanding officers of the Royal Navy. London's people line the wharves and bridges, watching solemnly as the procession passes by.

With the barge in sight the powerful guns blast into life from the Tower, drowning out the melodies drifting off the water. The river glitters with rich multi-coloured flags which sway in time with the rhythm of the tide.

Nelson will spend the night in the Admiralty as the city prepares for the final journey to St Paul's cathedral where the hero of the seas will rest for eternity.

The famous Horatio Nelson was born on 29th September 1758 at the rectory in the village of Burnham Thorpe in Norfolk. His father Edmund was a respectable man following the calling of the clergy. His mother Catherine née Suckling gave birth to eleven children of whom Horatio was the sixth. A somewhat sickly child, he was baptised twice, the first time at just few days old as it was feared he would not live.

Having been a pupil at the Paston School in North Walsham and King Edward VI's Grammar School in Norwich, Nelson was well educated. However, his schooldays were cut short when on Boxing Day 1767 his mother Catherine tragically and unexpectedly died. This left Edmund to care for their eight surviving children aged fourteen to just a few months.

In order to assist Edmund, his brother-in-law Captain Maurice Suckling took his young nephew on to his ship where he was officially received into the Navy in January 1771 as a midshipman aboard HMS Raisonnable.

Nelson was born to succeed and it is said that in his "heart and head he was all that heroes are made of".

His maternal name Suckling ensured that his mates had much pleasure in teasing him but Nelson was destined to prove he was no un-weaned child.

No sooner had Nelson been appointed midshipman than he commenced with his officer training, rising through the ranks while serving in the West Indies, the Baltic and Canada.

In March 1787 whilst on the island of Nevis he met and married Frances (Fanny) Nisbet at her home on the Montpelier Estate.

With his quick grasp of strategy, in January 1793 he was given the command of HMS Agamemnon and Britain entered into the French revolutionary wars.

Nelson was placed in charge of operations against the French who were occupying the island of Corsica. He spent seven months fighting ashore and in July that year whilst examining one of his batteries he was hit in the eye by debris from a sandbag burst by enemy fire. He went on to lose all vision in his right eye but he did not have it removed and refused to wear a patch.

A month later the French-occupied Corsican fortress of Calvi fell and at the later battle of Copenhagen Nelson, famous for not following orders, put his telescope to his blind eye stating "I really do not see the signal".

In 1797 his usual defiance of orders actually helped win the battle of Cape St Vincent. Next, he attacked Santa Cruz de Tenerife where he was wounded on his right arm, leading to its amputation. Forced to return to England Nelson formally separated from his wife in favour of his mistress Emma Hamilton with whom he later fathered an illegitimate child, Horatia.

By 1801 Nelson had risen to be Vice Admiral, leading to his escalating involvement in the conflict of the Napoleonic wars against France.

In 1802 Nelson was awarded an honorary degree of law by the University of Oxford.

21st October 1805 marked the fateful battle of Trafalgar where at around 1.15 p.m. whilst on board the HMS Victory Nelson took a bullet from a French sniper as he was pacing the quarter deck. The musket shot struck Nelson on his left shoulder with such force that he was thrown to his knees. The shot smashed through bone and tore through muscle, piercing his lung and severing an artery in its path. Nothing could be done to save Nelson's life and in the hours preceding his death, he left commands to his crew and messages of love to his family. He lived long enough to hear of their victory. Nelson's last words, witnessed by three members of his crew, were said to be "Thank God I have done my duty".

Following his death Nelson's body was placed in a cask of brandy mixed with camphor and myrrh for preservation and was transported to

Gibraltar, arriving on 28th October 1805. The brandy was then replaced with spirits of wine.

His body arrived at the Royal Hospital for Seaman in Greenwich on 23rd December 1805 where it was transferred to a lead-lined coffin. He stayed there until the 5th January, lying in state for the final three days.

More than 15,000 people came to the event, where distressing scenes occurred, caused by the opening of the wrong gates (the carriage side gates). This negligence led to a number of avoidable incidents. As the narrow wickets were opened at 8.00 a.m., hundreds of people pushed from the rear. This caused those at the side to be crushed, including a baby killed in its mother's arms. Those at the front were knocked down and trampled as the crowd surged forwards. On old woman "literally had her nose scraped from her face". The guards, though numerous and vigilant, could scarcely control the crowd who pushed for admittance.

On 8th January 1806 Nelson was taken up the Thames to Whitehall Steps to stay overnight at the Admiralty.

At eleven o'clock the following morning Nelson, covered with black velvet adorned with his coat of arms, headed for St Paul's Cathedral. He was accompanied by thirty-two admirals including chief mourner the Admiral of the Fleet, Sir Peter Parker, and over a hundred captains, with eight hundred soldiers and twenty thousand volunteers lining the streets. In the funeral carriage decorated with the carved image of the head and stern of his ship HMS Victory and surrounded by escutcheons (coats of arms), Nelson began his final journey.

The ceremony ran for over four hours and many hymns were sung, including "Lord, let me know mine end". Finally, members of the Royal Navy ceremonially folded and placed the flag from HMS Victory on the tomb. However, in a sickening twist the flag was then torn to pieces by the sailors desperate for mementos to sell to the public. Fragments can be found in both private and public museums all over the world.

Nelson was then interred within a sarcophagus originally carved for the executed Tudor cardinal, Thomas Wolsey.

Numerous monuments have been dedicated to Nelson's memory the most famous being Nelson's Column in Trafalgar Square. Built between 1840-1843 the monument cost £47,000, an equivalent of more than six million pounds today (2022). The Russian Tsar (Alexander I) paid a quarter of the bill himself whilst numerous private investors donated to the project. It's been estimated that fifteen million people visit the monument per year.

4. THOMAS CLARKSON

It's June, 1785

In Wadesmill, Hertfordshire, a man deep in thought dismounts his horse and angrily slumps down on the grassy verge. He has come to a conclusion, one that will completely dominate his life, transform opinions and alter the course of world history.

Thomas Clarkson was born on 28th March 1760 in Wisbech, Cambridgeshire, the son of John and Ann Ward. His father, a clergyman and teacher at Wisbech Grammar School, died when Thomas was just six years old.

An excellent student, he studied at the local Grammar School and St Paul's School in London, gradually becoming a serious, devout man.

In 1779 he attended St John's College, Cambridge where in 1785, he won a university essay prize on the thoroughly researched topic entitled 'Is it right to make slaves of others against their will?' Whilst researching he became disgusted by the accounts and developed a lifelong goal of abolishing the slave trade.

Over the next seven years he was to ride 35,000 miles, taking him as far as Paris.

He began to collect evidence for his speeches, enough to convince others to turn against the vile practice of slavery.

He interviewed 20,000 witnesses mainly sailors of the slave trading ships, collecting stories to share in his work.

In June 1786 his essay was published, making him a well-known figure in public politics. He began to meet other political figures intent on making a difference. They formed a committee for the abolition of the African slave trade enabling him to approach a young William Wilberforce who came on board. He continued to gather evidence of ill treatment and examples of equipment like shackles and branding irons used on slaves.

Such was Thomas' influence he was attacked in Liverpool by eight or nine sailors who attempted to drown him, but he knocked one down and made a hasty escape.

Over the next five months he rode from town to town giving speeches to all who would listen but sadly Wilberforce's first bill was defeated in Parliament. However, public opinion was shifting and 300,000 people were boycotting West Indian sugar.

On 20th January 1796 at Bury St Edmunds Thomas was married to a Catherine Buck and later that year they welcomed his only son John to the world.

Clarkson continued his mission although his health began to fail.

Finally, on 25th March 1807 the Act for the Abolition of the Slave Trade was passed, meaning that any British captain caught with slaves on board was fined £10 for every one.

Over the years Thomas purchased Playford Hall, Suffolk and continued his task, gaining the freedom of the city of London.

In 1833, a huge victory for all involved, the Slavery Abolition Act was passed giving all British slaves the freedom they so deserved.

At four o'clock in the morning of 26th September 1846 Thomas Clarkson passed away in Playford Hall.

He is buried close by in the local church of St Mary's.

It is estimated that eleven million Africans were forced to board ships transporting them to the Caribbean and America. Roughly 9.6 million survived to be sold into enslavement on plantations and households by mainly European settlers.

5. WILLIAM CALCRAFT

It's Saturday, 25th August 1860

A train stands still at the platform, waiting to expel its passengers. Groups of shabbily dressed people push and shove each other trying to be the one to catch the first glimpse of the infamous 'Jack Ketch'. A door is pushed wide and a stout man with dark hair speckled with grey alights. His guards' arms are extended as they push back the rowdy lot allowing him to pass. Once out of the station he strolls down the lane with a carpet bag in one hand packed with a white cap and a length of rope half an inch round. Once at his destination, he glances at the chapel clock, passes his bag to the waiting warden and buries his gnarly hands into his black trouser pockets. Calmly and leisurely and despite the ruckus all around, he quietly passes through the open door and goes into the waiting dark. The crowd, now numbering in their thousands, awaits, in constant competition to be the ones at the front. The bell chimes noon as the sad procession begins its short journey over the cold grey flagstoned yard. Now taking the lead he climbs upwards as they boo and hiss. Next, follow two priests and guards who between them are steadying the condemned man. His arms are pinioned by a large brown leather belt. Once arrived, the man glances up at the sky, noting the dark clouds dominating the blue. In his hands is the rope, made of hemp by skilful workmen. He throws it twice round the cross beam, loops the end and lets it fall to the platform as the accused extends a trembling arm to shake his hand. With cap and loop in hand he expertly pulls one after the other over the shaking man's head. The priests have not halted in their prayers as the lever is pulled. The platform splits, dropping the man into the wide space below. Swinging round and round, the convicted writhes with convulsions as the rabble let out a low groan. The man, noticing a slight error, calmly steadies the swing with one finger applied on the shoulder below him. Within two to three minutes the struggle is over as the victim sways in the breeze. The sky breaks, sending fat drops of rain onto the ground and down the face of the bearded executioner. They wait for the body to stop convulsing. The legs continue to twitch giving the cruel illusion he still lives. The crowds disperse as the clock chimes one and the corpse is placed in a black coffin. It's over. He is thinking of his lunch as he waits for his pay.

William Angus Calcraft, was born in Little Baddow, Essex to labouring parents William and Sarah. He was baptised at the Independent Chapel on 12th November 1800. Having no formal education and no school friends he did not learn in the normal fashion but he was still taught to read and write. Sadly, however, he knew little of how to socialise with others. He became a quiet kindly man described by some as a gentle and simple soul.

Before 1818 he moved to London, both homeless and penniless, but he managed to teach himself the trade of a cobbler as well as selling meat pies around Newgate prison, barely earning enough to survive. After meeting John Foxton, the resident hangman at Newgate Goal, he was offered the position as assistant and was in charge of public floggings, using both cat o' nine tails and a birch rod with little effect on his sensibilities. Both professional and blunt he was invited to assist 'Old Tom Cheshire' or 'Cheese' and Foxton as deputy hangman responsible for helping with the execution of the condemned.

In the early 19th century, anybody could become a hangman by simply applying to the prison commissioner and over two hundred and fifty people did so every year. After separating the mad from the sane, a medical examination had to be passed and a week's training completed. The successful had to witness an execution, assisting if required. Next their names were added to a list made available to all sheriffs. However new people would rarely be picked as the experienced would always be the first choice for the hideous job.

Foxton died on 14th February 1829 and within a month Calcraft was sworn in as London's official executioner. He was paid between twenty-five and thirty shillings a week plus £3 a quarter and had full permission to take possession of clothes or belongings after the task. He also rather strangely stayed within the home of the condemned (which must have been awkward for the family).

With the advent of the railway, he travelled the country performing for a guinea and the cost of a first-class ticket. This turned out to be beneficial as an Act of Parliament was amended stopping executions for larceny, robbery and forgery which together formed over eighty percent of all convictions) He was even accused of selling inch-long pieces of rope to the onlookers for five shillings a piece. This turned out to be false as when sworn under oath he admitted to using a rope again and again after testing its strength. This is where the expression money for old rope is derived from. He was used to being too thrifty to use a new rope each time. He is also remembered as prolonging the suffering of criminals using the short drop method, although this is unfair as the new long drop method was not even invented until after his death.

On 19th April 1824 he married Louisa Kingsbury back in Essex and by 1827 welcomed his first surviving child William. Becoming a family man, he was often seen gardening and was particular attracted to flowers of rare varieties.

After an incident where one man's arms became free and delayed his death, Calcraft invented a leather belt with wrist straps in order to pinion the arms completely.

In 1850 I found him appearing in court for failing to provide financial support for his mother who had been forced to enter the workhouse and claim help from the parish. It is noted in the papers how gentle and loving he was towards her, a surprise to those who did not know him. In

1869 he is in court again being sued for not paying his bill by a landlord, who called him a mean man. Calcraft replied wittily with "I was born too near a wood to be frightened by an owl!" after which The Pall Mall printed how it was evident that hangmen had yet to undergo a civil service examination!

Another event by which his character was forever tainted was one occasion where, as he pulled up the lever, a doubly unfortunate fellow fell through the trap onto his feet below. An inquest was held where it became clear that this was a new rope which had snapped. The jury found, however, that on this occasion it was accidental. Which was bound to happen some time as in his career he executed up to 450 individuals including thirty-four women.

After the capital punishment act of 1868 all executions had to be in private, ending the entertainment somehow so popular with the thousands who turned out at each hanging. Calcraft performed the last public and first private executions, working till his seventies even though he was forced to take on an assistant when his hands began to shake. He died in 1879 leaving his wife and three children.

I found evidence that Calcraft was a perfect gentleman when not working, and he was polite and professional performing his job with an indifference that came from so much experience. Lastly, the rumour that he would hasten deaths by climbing on the shoulders or pulling on the legs of the victim seems also to be unverified, although I spent many hours trying to find evidence of this claim. My conclusion is that others may have done so but he seemed not to have done this as not one newspaper of the time which I read mentioned any failures in his role other than the unfortunate accident that I described. History has remembered Calcraft as mean, nasty and unloving to his mother. A man who bungled job after job prolonging the torture of the accused. It seems he is doomed to forever be tainted and thought of as exactly what people would expect from a professional executor rather than the truth. I found this truly sad and hope by writing this this I can change this fact, one person at a time.

6. HOWARD CARTER

It's Sunday, 26th November 1922 - 2.00 p.m.

A man dressed in cotton shirt and trousers which are dusty from the sandy ground leads three others down the steep steps to a passage carved into the rock. He stops at a door decorated with cartouches of a familiar king. With a sharp trowel in his hand, he loosens the blockage around the top left-hand corner. Once the hole is cut, foul scented air billows through into the passage in which they stand. The three others behind are deathly silent, bubbling with excitement at the possibilities ahead. He lifts his candle upwards and waits for the dust to settle. Once his vision becomes accustomed to the dimness he gasps in wonder. He widens the hole and stares ahead, noting the glistening gold-encrusted objects. Chariots, vases and gilded chests shine in the single flickering flame. The man directly behind him whispers "Can you see anything?" He replies in a muted tone "Yes, it is wonderful ". Finally, after many years spent searching, they had found the tomb of the boy king Tutankhamun surrounded by a multitude of extraordinary and beautiful objects that still have the same effect now as before, when the chamber first was sealed three thousand years ago. The man, Howard Carter, spent the next ten years photographing, sketching and identifying the precious artefacts brought from under the ground, stored at Cairo Museum and later uncovered for the awaiting public.

Howard Carter was born on 9th May 1874. He was the youngest of the eleven children of Samuel Carter and Martha née Sands. Carter was born in Kensington, a sickly child not completely expected to live past infancy. Whilst still very young he was moved to the Norfolk countryside, to Swaffham, where he was home-schooled under the guidance of an aunt in the fresh countryside air, free of pollution.

Carter had a talent for art inherited from his father who sketched animals for a living. Under close supervision Carter was taught the fundamentals, surpassing his father's talent at a young age.

Once on a visit with his father to meet William Amherst at his home, Didlington Hall, Carter discovered the Egypt rooms packed with ancient artefacts collected over the years. He was so inspired that he accepted an offer from the egyptologist Percy Newberry to assist him on an archaeological dig. Carter's job was that of apprentice tracer where he could inspect and touch artefacts thousands of years old. He was just seventeen years old. Later that year Carter got an opportunity to work alongside another famous egyptologist Flinders Petrie, which he took without much thought. Whilst under Petrie's instruction Carter learnt the skills to become an archaeologist. As he grew in experience the wonder of the job never left him and he went on to discover the Temple of Queen Hatshepsut among many others.

Eight years after his arrival in Alexandria, Carter was offered the role of Inspector General of Monuments for Upper Egypt. However, his stubborn personality often saw him at war with others around him, leading his superiors to limit his work and eventually to Carter's resignation.

Carter worked for a time as a guide and commercial artist until one day he was introduced to Lord Carnarvon who saw promise in Carter and agreed to finance the search for Tutankhamun within the Valley of the Kings.

In 1914 the outbreak of war stopped all excavations but Carter would not be beaten and as soon as the war was over, funded by Carnarvon, he began the search for the boy king.

After three years Carnarvon was losing all hope in the search, which meant that Carter had to plead for more time which he was granted, just one last season. One day in November 1922 a young boy playing with a stick in the sand discovered a step cut into the rock. The boy alerted Carter to the find and he told all members of the team to put aside their current work and begin the painstaking job of excavating through sand and gravel to uncover the steps. At the bottom there was a door leading to an antechamber where another sealed door, once opened, revealed the famous treasure taken into the afterlife with King Tutankhamun.

In the week before the extraordinary discovery Carter had bought a canary and its premature death, eaten by a cobra on the day that the tomb was opened, and that of Lord Carnarvon in April 1923 led the workers to fear the curse of the pharaohs was to blame. Carnarvon died from septicemia from a mosquito bite. Over the next twelve years eight of the fifty-two strong team died unexpectedly.

Carter was not thrilled with the attentions of the press, having gone from unknown to infamous overnight.

In 1932 after thirty years in Egypt, Carter finished all the conservation work and sailed home to England. There he travelled giving speeches to the public who could not get enough of the Egyptian history resulting from the find.

In March 1939, after becoming the world's first celebrity archaeologist, Carter died unmarried from cancer, reinforcing beliefs that the curse had claimed one final victim.

7. VIOLET LEE

It's Sunday, 1st September 1940 - 5.30 a.m.

A lady dressed in a matching jacket and skirt covered by a long fur coat with turned back cuffs stands under the clock, shoulders back, head tilted upwards. Beside her, her seven-year-old twin boys stand struggling in the crowds to stay near her. They are being watched closely by an older boy. All three share a likeness typical of brothers. Never-ending lines of children fill the platforms, gas masks hanging by their waists, sewn-on white labels flutter in the breeze attached to coats, each with their names printed neatly in black ink. The noise is deafening, trains departing, children sobbing held tightly by teachers who have become mothers that day. A woman similar in age leans over and in her broad cockney accent asks the question on all their minds, "Do you know where we are going then, love? She replies with a sharp single "No".

On board the train the twins, forgetting their manners, are becoming restless. The conductor announces that they've reached their destination, Ipswich. They disembark and follow the crowds outside to the waiting buses where, on boarding, she ensures the boys go first. Once settled they slowly begin their journey into the unknown.

They arrive and are finally told they have been billeted to Hadleigh a small market town. Holding onto the youngest boys she's pushed towards iron cattle pens in the market square where they are picked out like animals one by one. After a few minutes a well-dressed respectable couple approach and the gentleman in his smart suit and polished leather shoes simply states "I'll take these ones".

After a short walk they are shown into a red brick mansion and introduced to Dr and Mrs Styles. Amazed by the inside bathroom with hot running water even the boys are silent but not for long.

Violet Annie Lee, was born on 5th August 1909 at 33 Chapman Road, Hackney, to Jimmy Lee and Mary née Houghton.

Jimmy was known locally as Southpaw Cannonball Lee. Born in 1876, he was a street entertainer where to wow the crowds he would walk across broken beer bottles, put out red hot pokers on his tongue, sing and play music on various instruments. He is recorded as stating the poker had to be red hot or it would hurt!

Violet's grandfather Lee was a famous boxer of Romany descent. He had violent epileptic seizures, leading to him attacking family members and as a result he was taken to Long Grove Asylum in Epsom where he remained for the rest of his life. Jimmy was so deeply affected that he remained teetotal for life.

Violet was a rebellious young woman who lied about her age to marry Charles Kray in July 1926 at Kingsland Road registry office, with his friend and neighbour Harry Hopwood as a witness. At the time she knew she was four months pregnant. Her family were so outraged they did not communicate until they met their first grandson in March 1927.

In March 1929 Violet fell pregnant again and gave birth in December to a girl named Violet. Sadly, she died just hours after birth devastating her mother and causing her to fall into a deep depression. A doctor told Charlie senior "if she failed to fall pregnant again, she would fade". Reggie in his book 'Reggie Kray's East End stories' writes how he found a dried carnation from Violet's funeral wreath after his mother's death.

Happily, Violet gave birth to twins on 24th October 1933 in Hoxton, East London, first came Reginald and ten minutes later Ronald. She adored her boys and they in turn adored her, taking her side in every family fall out and treating her with the utmost respect at all times.

In 1939 the family moved from Sterne Street to the infamous 178 Vallance Road, Bethnal Green where they lived happily in the labyrinth of dark and dismal streets named the slums. Violet's family all lived close by, so many in fact that locally the area was called "Lee Corner" and the road as "Fort Vallance". Charlie later built a gym in the back room so he could spend extra time training the boys to box. The area is described as blackened with the grime of a century, a home for London's top crooks and home of poor families. Poverty kept the tallyman going and mid-week before payday you could see the queues outside the pawnbrokers. Children roamed the street at night working as errand boys in the breeding-ground of tearaways and criminals.

The boys were educated at Wood Close School in Brick Lane then Daniel Street School where their teacher described them as the salt of the earth.

Violet's husband Charlie senior, not wanting to go to war, deserted from the army and was on the run for twelve years until the queen signed an amnesty. The boys found it ironic that it was the same year they went on the run from the army.

In 1940, Violet and all three boys were evacuated to Hadleigh, Suffolk where despite Mrs Styles' best efforts they refused to be educated and would not learn to read. A glimpse of the violence in their character was shown when they killed Dr Styles' cockerel for fun. Despite this they had fond memories of Suffolk and sledging down Constitution Hill, fighting the locals, apple scrumping and spending hours with Charlie (when he was not working in the chippy) as he coached them in boxing. After a year in the country Violet was missing her friends and family and took the boys back to Vallance Road. They were devastated and never forgot their love for Suffolk and its locals where they were treated so well without fear or malice as was the case when they were older. They later reminisce about scouring the woods and fields for hours, revelling in the fresh air and the boundless freedom of country life.

In 1948, Reggie won the Hackney schoolboys' boxing championship, the London schoolboy and the London juniors titles. The following year he was arrested and charged with GBH but the charges did not stick.

In 1951, the boys were called up for National Service and following in their father's footsteps they were not going quietly. When they arrived to "sign up" Ronnie punched the corporal who attempted to stop them leaving! As a result, they became the last prisoners in the Tower of London. This marked the beginning of all three boys' arrests, charges and convictions, spending time in prisons all over the United Kingdom. Amusingly (as Ronnie was not great at doing time) Reggie would go to prison and serve his brother's sentence for him!

By 1957, the boys had built an empire called The Firm from their snooker club in Bethnal Green, taking part in organised criminal activities in London.

Violet still adored her boys, visiting them in prison wherever they were stating that she loved the little monsters. Violet having been bought up within the lifestyle, she couldn't be blamed for the boys turning out the way they did. She would have visitors who would lay out stolen wares on the kitchen table as she examined and bought them. She encouraged their boxing careers and supported them in their activities. She even sewed the razor blades into their lapels (razor gangs were common from the 1920s onwards). They grew up seeing her hiding Charlie senior from the wardens and socialising with all the well-known criminal characters. They were always surrounded by the underworld so it's only natural they followed the example.

The Krays owned many of the top clubs in London and rubbed shoulders with all the celebrities of the times, such as Diana Dors and Judy Garland. Reggie even dated Barbara Windsor and Ronnie had a relationship with Lord Boothby. Violet never had any problems with Ronnie's sexuality and his father simply ignored the fact.

During all this time Ronnie's behaviour became more of a concern to the family. He had mood swings, would refuse to eat, shave only one side of his face and went from sitting completely still for hours to violent frenzies. Worryingly he was not the first in the family with mental health problems and later in life he was officially diagnosed with schizophrenia.

At the Krays' peak in 1965, Reggie married Frances O'Shea at St James' Church in Bethnal Green. Her family were against the match and her mother wore all black at the wedding.

On 9th March 1966 in the Blind Beggar, Whitechapel Road, Ronnie shot George Cornell, a member of the rival gang the Richardsons. Things were getting out of hand with Ronnie's mental health.

Continuing with their love for Suffolk the boys bought Violet a pink house next to the post office in Bildeston and a big house called The Brooks close by for themselves. The locals tell tales of them giving children donkey rides and giving out money for ice creams.

Sadly Frances, no stranger to a life of addiction and crime, committed suicide in June 1967. Just months later in October Reggie stabbed Jack "The Hat" Mc Vitie in the stomach. Knowing they had limited time as free men they fled to Suffolk to hide at Gedding Hall (later Bill Wyman's home), close to Bury St Edmunds and to their own home, The Brooks. They were arrested by Detective Chief Superintendent Leonard "Nipper" Read of the Metropolitan Police in May 1968, convicted of murder and jailed for life.

Violet visited both boys regularly and on one occasion when she was presented with two jewellery boxes made by a prisoner, she said they were truly beautiful and "Trust them to remember their mum" She still referred to them as her beautiful boys. As her health faded and she had a stay in hospital there were always two huge bouquets, one from each of the twins.

Violet Kray died of a heart attack on 4th August 1982 in her Bunhill Row flat, Shoreditch. On 11th August crowds collected outside the flat with wreaths being laid in front. Charles senior died seven months later. They were married for over fifty years. Both are buried at Chingford Mount Cemetery, Section number B8, Grave 70707.

Both the boys were allowed to attend their mother's funeral service but not the burial. Ronnie died of a heart attack in Broadmoor Hospital in 1995 and Reggie, released from Wayland Prison on compassionate grounds, died of cancer six years later in October 2000. They, too, are buried at Chingford Mount with Frances and all the family close to each other.

CHAPTER FIVE

East Anglian Tales

1. THE BLACK SHUCK

It's 4th August 1577 - 9.00 a.m.

Picture a quiet Suffolk village, thatched stone cottages line the street leading to an ancient church built in 1160. The sky is blue, not a cloud in sight as the locals stream into the porch and take their places either side of the aisle. The rector stands at the front sharing his wisdom with the gathered followers of Christ. As they strain to hear his sermon the light begins to fade. From the windows they can see the sky fill with black, casting a solid darkness in the room. The flock begin to panic as the clouds burst, sending violent raindrops falling like rapids. Hailstones the size of cannonballs shatter the coloured window glass, pieces exploding onto the parishioners' heads. Blazes of light illuminate the space showing them cowering, protecting their young from the violent scene. With a roar of thunder and flash of fire the heavy oak door springs open to reveal the devil himself. In the form of a hound some seven feet tall he gallops through the church wringing the necks of two of the flock kneeling down offering prayer. With a blood-curdling howl the hellish monster flies, tearing and mutilating flesh with razor-edged teeth and sharp, bloodied claws. In a puff of smoke, he vanishes, leaving the rector to calm his troubled flock.

Twelve miles away in a similar church the storm rages on, the terrified locals huddle together as a beast as big as a horse jumps down from a beam and prowls up to the altar. As a bolt of lightning crashes into the church, mysterious burns fry human skin whilst the devil rips and tears his passage through, bringing down the vestry wall. With an enormous crash the steeple collapses sending stone shattering onto those below. As quick as he came the beast vanishes, leaving the sulphurous scent of brimstone in his wake. Locals will tell the tale for hundreds of years to come of the 'strange and terrible wundur' that visited Suffolk that day.

That terrible wonder was the legend of the devil's hound, "Black Shuck". The word Shuck derives from the old English word Scucca the "Devil's

Fiend" from the root word to Skuch, to terrify. His appearance alters from the size of a big dog to that of a horse. Sometimes he's a cyclops with one red glistening eye, other times with two eyes the size of saucers shining red and sharp teeth, foaming at the mouth. Always with a black shaggy coat so shiny you could see your reflection.

The Reverend Abraham Flemming, rector of St Mary's church, Bungay (the first church in our tale) documented a huge thunderstorm in which two people died. He writes of a huge black dog running around the church with "great swiftness".

At Holy Trinity Church, Blythburgh (the second church in our tale) you can still see the scorch marks of the devil on the huge carved door. These mysterious marks can be explained. After the Reformation the church was used as a stable and a farrier's shop; could the scorch marks be those of the red-hot poker used to shoe horses? As for the mention of terrible burns, could these not be expected inside a building struck several times by lightning? However modern minds explain this away, to these people a storm was sent by the devil. With very little scientific knowledge, this event viewed only by candlelight and flashes of lightning sent shadows across the church. To them this tale had no other explanation. Add this to the fact the occasion was documented by a holy man who they trusted would tell the truth. With the Reformation sweeping through Britain the church was desperate to keep the people on the right path of the original faith. Was this a story told by desperate Catholic churchmen to keep their flock from straying? This we cannot know. However, the Black Shuck is an East Anglian folk tale carried over the years with its origin said to be from the Vikings who settled here in the east. To them the howling heard in the whistling wind was the howling of the black hound of Odin. When Eric Blood-Axe sailed around Scotland to settle in the Isle of Man the Moddey Dhoo was born, their shuck. Each county has its own Black Dog stories.

Dogs appear in folklore from ancient times, for example the three-headed Cerberus in Greek mythology guarding the entrance of Hades, the underworld, so no soul could escape. Then we have the Egyptian deity Anubis, the jackal-headed God used in funerary rites in those times and found adorning the walls of many burial chambers and temples on sites along the Nile.

Archaeological evidence from the Roman period also sees the notion of dogs guarding entrances with the discovery of the remains of sixteen dogs inside a well at Staines, near London. These were documented as having been an offering to water gods made when the well ran dry.

Dogs were also associated with improving health as Roman paintings show illustrations of healing deities often being depicted with a dog as a companion.

In British folklore we have The Grim, a black dog with red eyes known to make nocturnal visits to foretell death.

Shuck's story is documented in 1127 in the Anglo-Saxon Chronicles where Henry of Poitou, Abbot of Peterborough, writes of local tales of big black and loathsome hunters riding black horses through the woods, sounding their ghostly horns into the night. He wrote that twenty or thirty stayed in the area over fifty days. This story named the "wild hunt" was retold all over Europe. Was it a fact or was it a tale of caution to keep people indoors and away from the woods so as not to freeze to death? Could it also have been told to keep those from disturbing poachers robbing their master's fowl?

In 1190 Walter Map, a medieval writer, documents the legend of Wild Edric in the Clun area of the Marches, the Welsh borderlands, who was said to haunt the hills around Church Stretton, Shropshire in the form of a large black dog.

In 1300 the Shuck appears again to a healthy young boy going about his daily duties at Bungay castle. The tale from here on out tells of the sighting of the beast being connected to imminent death, as the boy died later that day. Is this another cautionary tale to keep children from approaching strange dogs? Each story features the same big black dog portraying death for many years.

In Essex, Shuck patrols the lonely coastal roads and ancient pathways. Could the legend be used here by local smugglers (fond of creating stories) trying to keep away the locals so they could spirit away their goods with little disruption? Other places often guarded by these vicious devil hounds were local graveyards. This could have been spread into lore by resurrectionists, desperate to make money by digging up reasonably fresh corpses to sell on to medicine men in hospitals and universities.

In Clopton Green near Stowmarket, Shuck (now headless) guarded gold at Clopton Hall in the form of a terrifying man-dog hybrid who was known to stalk the site where St Felix of Burgundy had buried his treasure. In Norfolk he is also said to resemble a werewolf howling in the wild winds as they scream through the trees.

Other historic references of dogs in folklore see them as the protector, leading lost people safely off the lonely moors and fens and there are many references to these mysterious ghostly hounds guarding gates, stiles and other entrances such a river paths and bridges.

Some dog-related lore has even made its way into medieval medicine and then into phrases used to this day. Before antiseptics and antibiotics, a dog bite could well kill you. However, the cure back then was to fry the hair of the dog that bit you and place on the wound with a sprig of rosemary, hence the well-known saying "the hair of the dog."

Dogs have been said to have the power of second sight for thousands of years, seeing ghosts and even foretelling things such as the weather. For example, a dog eating grass meant it was sure to rain!

Linked to sightings of big shaggy dogs are the ongoing sightings of big cats especially in the 1980-90s with the well-known story of the "Beast of Bodmin" where a panther-like creature prowled the moorlands in Cornwall. There, being so many sightings, the government ordered an official investigation into the matter but unfortunately this ended with no results.

It is easily done to take these stories with a pinch of salt and discount them as stories to scare people away or teach lessons to children but these stories are told in different towns and villages all over western Europe and have been told from ancient times up to most recent in May 2020 in Wales. These cannot be explained to date.

However, I have a theory about our Black Shuck of 1577:

In 2015 a "DigVentures" archaeological investigation, fronted by Time Team's one and only Racksha Dave, was organized at Leiston Abbey, south of Bungay, for the general population to experience archaeology in the field. They unexpectedly uncovered a huge skeleton of a dog, which would have stood seven feet tall on its hind legs. Carbon dating placed this creature's death at around the same time as the attacks on Bungay and Blythborough churches. This dog was buried with care in a shallow grave inside the abbey kitchens and identified as a Great Dane. Is it possible that a local abbot's beloved hunting dog, knowing its routes between churches, went rabid? Could he, in searching for his master, have caused the distressing scenes in limited light as experienced in the churches nearby? Once again, we will never know the truth behind Old Shuck of 1577 but I hope with stories like these he will go on being part of British folklore for many years yet.

2. THE WITCH FINDERS

It's Sunday, 27th August 1645

In the bustling town of Bury St Edmunds eighteen terrified, innocent men and women stand upon the gallows, the stiff nooses looped around their necks, hands bound, resigned to their fate.

John Stearne was born in 1610, in Long Melford, Suffolk into a well-educated, wealthy, Puritan family. A member of the gentry, Stearne was a landlord renting to farmers and respectable families within Lawshall and Manningtree in East Anglia.

The seventeenth century could well be seen as the bleakest era of English history. Plague and death haunted the land. Riots broke out in many towns and Catholics and witches were seen as a form of disease, to be cut out to protect the godly. In 1642, the country broke out into civil war. The chaos that ensued meant the justices of the peace were now responsible for convictions. Just a few years before William Dowsing, a Suffolk man, had tramped around the country smashing stained glass and decorations that were seen as idolatrous. Religion was the cause of much strife.

Puritans at the time believed that by swearing 'we do rob God of his honour' and that 'God abhorreth liars and hath reserved great torment for them' and Stearne was a devout Puritan.

Many people believed in ghosts and a larger number had superstitions, omens or charms. Mummified cats, silver coins, horseshoes and skulls were built into walls and chimneys to ward off evil.

In Bury St Edmunds in 1644 Stearne married local girl Agnes Cawston and soon afterwards his first child was born. Come March 1645, after discovering a coven of witches in Manningtree, Essex, Stearne received a warrant allowing him to search their homes and interrogate the suspects. Matthew Hopkins, ten years his junior, volunteered to assist him. Over the next three years the duo directed the torture of hundreds of men and women accused of witchcraft.

In the summer of 1645, Stearne and Hopkins arrived in Brandeston, Suffolk and begun to round up suspects. One of these was an eighty-year-old minister called John Lowes. Generally disliked by his flock, he was a contentious man who had served his community for forty-eight years, making many enemies. A year earlier the villagers had tried to condemn him as a witch but he retracted his confession. This time Lowes was brutally tortured. He was marched to the nearby moat at Framlingham Castle where the witchfinders tied his hands behind his back, wrapped him in a sheet and swum him. This was the practice of submerging the suspect in water. If they sank, they were innocent but if they floated, they were declared guilty. Ducking stools were also a common feature in the country village pond. Lowes was then taken back to his house and illegally tortured. Stearne stripped him naked and examined his body for the devil's mark. This was said to be where a witch's familiar sucked the blood of its host. A mole on his head and other blemishes were then poked with 3-inch spikes. Next Stearne and Hopkins tied him to a chair and began the process of Watching where he was kept awake for seven days. Lastly, they forced the minister to run on the spot for many hours with no sleep until he collapsed with exhaustion.

Eventually Lowes confessed to having six imps whom he ordered to sink a ship killing all sixteen men on board and to causing 'the child of Nathaniel Mann to languish and die'. He was found guilty and hanged with seven others.

In July 1645, based on Stearne's accusations a trial was held in Chelmsford where twenty-nine people were accused of witchcraft. Four died in diabolical conditions in prison, sixteen were hanged and nine reprieved.

Documentary evidence showed that at Stowmarket Stearne and Hopkins charged the local magistrates £23 for their services, the cost being so high that a local tax was levied in order to pay the fee. This would be the equivalent of £3,800 today (2022).

By this time other prominent people such as the Puritan cleric John Gaule were getting suspicious and serious questions were being asked. It was said that the witchfinders were operating purely for profit and public support soon began to wane. As a result, on 27th August 1647 Hopkins retired. Montague Summers, a clergyman and author, wrote in 1928 that 'his reign of terror has caused his name to stink in the nostrils of all decent persons ever since'.

Stearne continued on his own without success and the last inquisitions were in Ely, Cambridgeshire, in 1647. There was no further demand for the services of the witchfinders in England.

Hopkins died of tuberculosis on 12th August 1647 in Manningtree, Essex and was buried in the old churchyard at nearby Mistley, now destroyed. A year after his death Stearne published his only book "A confirmation and discovery of witchcraft".

Between 1653 and 1660 the retired witchfinder had five more children. Relying on inheritances he experienced a decline in wealth and went from being a gentleman to a yeoman.

Stearne lived in Lawshall until his death in 1670 and he is buried at the parish church there.

The Witchfinder General's methods spread to the new world colonies, where in May 1647 a Connecticut woman was hanged for being found guilty of witchcraft.

It was the first major American witch hunt in history. It would not to be the last and set the stage for the famous Salem Witch Trials in Massachusetts.

3. BARHAM WORKHOUSE

It's Thursday, 6th February 1851

A man weak from lack of sustenance shakes his purse and reaches inside. He feels for the coppers and shakes 2d into his calloused hand. He sighs as the realisation hits, not even enough for a loaf of bread. He has no other choice, he must go back to the workhouse he knows so well.

Edgar Ramplin, was baptised on 10th August 1834 in Crowfield, Suffolk. His mother, Rachel was unmarried.

In 1841, at just seven years old Edgar was left alone in the Bosmere and Claydon Union workhouse. Here in 1850, spurred on by a lack of food, fifty able-bodied men escaped from their ward and a riot ensued. Thankfully it was quickly bought under control.

Edgar entered the workhouse again in 1851, one of fifty who had sought shelter out of desperation that week. The workhouse was well over-populated and there was nowhere to sleep.

On Sunday 9th February, Edgar and the other inmates were sitting in silence devouring their tiny portions of bread. It's reported that a man shouted. Then from the other side of the partition a woman yelled in reply. Instantly around forty men began to attack the partition, shouting and breaking crockery. The children, terrified by the disturbance, started screaming and crying as they were ushered to safety by the schoolmaster.

A hundred and twenty able-bodied men, generally of good character, began to break benches, windows and even tear up the floor. At five o'clock Crisp Howard, the master of the workhouse, sent for the police. Whilst waiting for assistance the governor and porter were pelted with objects. Soon Police Inspector John Morgan, Constable James Moore and Constable Parr arrived and a battle began with Edgar and others fighting hand to hand for many minutes. Eventually the governor and police were overpowered and went into retreat to the bread room where they were followed. Windows and doors were broken and Mr. Howard and his party escaped through a window.

At that point Inspector Morgan was wounded in the eye by a brickbat which had been hurled, so seriously that he had to be put to bed.

The rioters following the police pelted them with missiles as they ran for their lives. The porter, George Carr was knocked down and kicked in the ribs. By 8.00 p.m. the inmates had full control of the building. Walls had been thrown down, paving stones pulled up and over a hundred windows were broken.

By 10.00 p.m. the troops of the 11th Hussars arrived from their barracks at Ipswich shouldering their guns in order to quieten the inmates, and fifty rioters were arrested.

On 29th March 1851 Edgar appeared in court charged with six indictments, assaulting police constables and the Police

Superintendent George Jukes. He was sentenced to one year's imprisonment with hard labour.

In the census that year he is listed at Ipswich County Gaol, St Margaret's, Suffolk.

For the next fifty years Edgar lived in Coddenham as a lodger in various public houses, always alone with no family.

He died in 1902 and is buried in the Bosmere District and in his will he left £9 3s 7d to a butter dealer, John Norman.

Workhouses came into being when Parliament passed the first poor relief act in 1564, allowing parish officers to house roaming beggars or vagrants.

Locally in Suffolk, an act of 1765 saw the Hundreds of Bosmere and Claydon incorporate thirty-five parishes overseen by a board of guardians.

The following year on the outskirts of Barham, Suffolk, a twenty-acre site was put aside to build a 'house of industry' and there a red brick H-shaped workhouse at the cost of £10,000 was built with accommodation for four hundred inmates.

On the first floor of each wing were wards for the sick with two rooms for women and three for men. At the front were lying-in rooms which were large and wide but dimly lit by one window. An isolation hospital stood apart at some distance at the end of Pest House Lane.

Paupers slept four to a bed on a straw mattress and were often overcrowded.

It was the opinion of the more 'well off' members of the public that this was the most economically acceptable way to deal with the poor. Jobs included spinning wool, sewing, knitting and making such things as were wanted in the family. The men were involved with domestic affairs.

In 1929 the Bosmere Union was an instructional centre set up by the Ministry of Labour for 'reconditioning' unemployed men who had 'gone soft by being out of work.' They were threatened with losing their benefits if they didn't attend.

In WW2 the building housed Italian prisoners of war.

It was demolished in 1963.

Barham workhouse was said to be the basis of Dickens' story Oliver Twist after he visited Suffolk and read the record book of a ten-year old apprentice.

4. THE GUN COTTON EXPLOSION

It's Friday, 11th August 1871 - 2.05 p.m.

A rumble is heard in Diss from seventeen miles away in Stowmarket. On land owned by the local Prentice family, a disastrous explosion has occurred.

The Stowmarket Guncotton Company, founded and owned by the Prentices, specialised in making gun cartridges using cotton dipped in various chemicals and washed in water. Built in 1863, it provided valuable employment to the local population.

Gun cotton was invented by German chemist Christian Schonbein in 1845. However, it was not till the 1860s that a process was developed by Frederick Abel that prevented the cotton from spontaneously combusting, enabling it to be used in the manufacturing of reliable firearm cartridges and cannon shot.

Just back from lunch, people were settling down to their daily grind. A deafening explosion ripped through the building sending a column of black smoke hundreds of feet in the air. A few minutes later another explosion ripped the tiles off roofs and smashed the fifteenth century windows of nearby Combs Church. Thirty miles away in Southwold, the shock of the explosion was felt as several tons of gun cotton ignited, leaving a crater 100ft across and 10ft deep.

Twenty-eight people died that day including children of just twelve years old and seventy-five more were injured. Over half those who died were young.

Struggling to save those injured, two members of the Prentice family were killed in the second blast.

An investigation followed, the first of its kind by any government, and a reward of £100 and a pardon were offered to any persons that came forward with viable reasons. The results concluded the cause to be a combination of the August hot weather and sabotage, and this led to the 1875 Explosives Act. To this day the reward stands.

It's 6th March 2014 and Vera Waspe, Stowmarket Town Mayor, heads a small group of people bunched together in the town's Old Cemetery as a memorial is unveiled.

After questions were raised by the public 140 years after that catastrophic day, local groups and businesses raised enough to money to pay for the memorial stone. Its engraving spells out the names of both adults and children who died in the disaster.

5. BORLEY RECTORY

It's Wednesday, 28th October 1937

In the centre of the room stands a bulky round table surrounded by people all focusing on one object. The room is dimly lit, so dark in fact that it's difficult to make out the features on the faces of those seated there. On the table a planchette, a heart-shaped object, sits upon three wheels with a pencil attached to it. Each person in the room waits with trepidation as the medium places two of her bony fingers on the plank. She breathes deeply, almost as in a trance. The silence, so imposing, creates an eerie foreboding presence, replaced by that of fear as a name is drawn out on the ouija, letter by letter. The medium creates large graphite marks that spell out the name, Mary [or Marie] Lairre. The woman asks questions in a low monotone voice and the story unfolds upon the white paper lining the table top. The entity explains that she was a nun living in Le Havre in France who, against her holy vows, fell hopelessly in love with a man bearing the name Waldegrave, a historic lord of the manor. As the planchette glides along, those listening hear how the man put his soft chubby hands around her neck and squeezed her breath and her life away. She spells out her request, a Catholic burial, a mass, some peace after three hundred years alone in a worthless place between heaven and burning hell. Trapped living her last moments over and over is a torture not deserved. Another question is greeted by the tortured silence once more, Mary has gone back to her prison between worlds. A man unfolding his long legs stands relighting the candles, It is all over, for today.

Within a little hamlet straddling the Suffolk border, a gloomy red brick mansion surrounded by tall trees stands, lonely and quiet within its imposing walls. Inside the narrow hallway the library waits, containing one gigantic wooden case against the papered walls. Books line the shelves in order of size, neatly awaiting their next avid reader to thumb through the crisp white pages, unlocking the secrets within. The land beside the church at Borley, in Essex has been inhabited many times. Once spelt Barley in Anglo-Saxon, the piece of land in question was first documented in the thirteenth century when Edward II granted the land to the Benedictine monks who built a monastery there. Around those times the wooden construction was replaced by a pretty little church that now bears the memorials of the Waldegrave family who hailed from Somerset and became lords of the manor, with a seat there for over three hundred years.

Much later an old rectory stood in place until 1841, when it was destroyed by fire. In 1863, the Reverend Henry Dawson Ellis Bull pulled down the remaining walls and built an imposing red brick mansion in the Gothic style of Augustus Welby Pugin. Surrounded by tall trees the neatly laid out gardens were dimly lit, creating a depressing atmosphere that along with the iron-barred windows of the kitchen and passages felt more like an institution than a home. Bull had a huge family of fourteen children, twelve surviving, so built an extension to house them all. With no electricity installed all lighting came from candles and oil lamps strategically placed around the rooms, mostly in front of huge gilded mirrors in order to reflect the light. Water came from a deep well in the central courtyard. Reverend Bull was in charge of the parish for thirty years. Tall and heavily built, Henry was a boxer in his youth and he loved shooting and hunting, a real country parson much entertained by the whispers and acoustic effects throughout the rectory. But the locals, already knowing the land to be haunted, stayed their distance and spread the tale relating to the 'Nuns Walk'.

Many years before, it is told, a monk from the monastery on the site fell sinfully in love with a nun from the nearby abbey at Bures. They made their escape in the middle of the night with the assistance of a lay brother. Whilst waiting for their horses and carriage they were captured and severely punished. The monk was hanged and the nun bricked up into a wall being constructed at her abbey. Imagine that, dying of lack of oxygen, no place to rest her weary body, nothing to drink, or eat, all alone. It's no wonder she is said to haunt the gardens, along with her phantom carriage and two headless horsemen, in a desperate search for her lover never to be found. It's unknown what punishment the lay brother was handed, maybe he is one of many restless souls haunting the church and village lanes?

One glorious June day the Bull family, home from a garden party, were in the grounds when Miss Ethel and her sisters Freda and Mabel clearly saw the figure of a nun floating slowly to the other side of the lawn. Ethel quickly sped inside to retrieve her other sister who was astonished, as the apparition had never been seen before in daylight. Many locals claim to have seen her, some asking who she was? Over a period of fifty years, twenty-odd witnesses reported to the Bull family about her presence stepping over a low stone wall and walking to the tree the other side of the lawn and fizzling away from sight. Walter Bull, who spent most of his life at sea, documented that he heard footsteps in the lane beside the rectory both day and night and had often hidden behind the ancient trees to catch his follower but to no avail. The locals all claim to have heard these steps and would never take the lane by the church at night. Henry Bull died in 1892 in the famous Blue Room, over the library, overlooking 'Nun's Walk'.

After his death the parish was passed to his son Harry who lived for another thirty-five years alongside his ghosts and romantic stories of dangerous love. Maids were reported to have seen a female figure who upon approaching vanished into thin air, causing such a fright they fainted. Harry also is reported as seeing a little man who hailed him from the lawn and ran off down the drive. He even had the main dining room window bricked up as he was tired of the spirits standing outside watching the family dine! The family were quite calm about their haunting even when the ladies were attacked in the night with slaps and poking. And then the footsteps along the hall stopping at the bedroom door and rapping three times. Harry even built a summer-house where he would sit smoking cigars waiting, calmly for activity to begin. In 1927 the Reverend Harry Bull died, once again in the Blue Room.

The next unlucky rector to live at Borley Rectory was Reverend Guy Smith who described his and his wife's two years in residence as "the darkest years of their life". Having been abroad working as a missionary he had no information regarding the hauntings. He was plagued by banging and sounds of furniture moving in the bedroom and no matter how many times they relocated the noises followed them, being much worse in the Blue Room or the kitchen. Within a week the spiral spring bells hanging below stairs started ringing, always when nobody stood in the rooms where the cord was being pulled. The phantom had a fascination with keys, they moved around and doors were locked and unlocked at will. No maid would stay longer than a week! And then came the gruesome discovery in the library where Mrs. Smith found a parcel. Carefully unwrapping it she revealed a human skull. Its origin was never discovered and the Bulls had no knowledge of it. Reverend Smith gave the dismembered head a good Christian burial in the churchyard over the lane.

Mrs. Smith possessed a small mirror on her dressing table in which the sound of tapping came. Even after leaving Borley to live in Cromer the sound would start in earnest. At their wits' end, Reverend Smith wrote to a local newspaper in search of a society which dealt in psychic matters to assist the couple. This unleashed an army of reporters and sightseers peeping through the windows and standing in the flowerbeds and they had to be contained by the police from the next town.

Even now, come 31st October, cars full of ghost hunters appear at the church in search of the rectory and its sprits. Visitors at first were welcomed by the locals. However, after constant vandalism and thoughtless littering they are less welcome today. One hot summer night, Reverend Smith, upon leaving the bedroom, heard the clear voice of a woman pleading "Don't, Carlos." After months of activity and an extreme effect on Mrs. Smith's mental health they left in August 1930, relocating to Long Melford. To his death he claimed "That house was a centre of some unknown and malign influence." Prior to this the famous psychical researcher Harry Price, having seen the article in the paper, was pressed to investigate. Price spent his entire career researching, writing and investigating the case; twenty years passed and never once did the proceedings become a bore.

After some time searching (due to the Rectory's public association with the paranormal) the Reverend Lionel Foyster, his wife Marianne and their adopted daughter took over the parish and moved into the Rectory. From October 1930 there began a period of five years of increasing violence and remarkable occurrences mostly directed at Marianne and all recorded by Price. The house seemed to be waking up as what began with footsteps upon the stairs and a vision of a tall man (later identified as the Reverend Bull) morphed into a full poltergeist haunting. Objects began to vanish and reappear in odd locations. At eleven o'clock one night, Reverend Foyster was in the bathroom when he heard his wife let out a blood-curdling scream. He bolted to her aid outside the Blue Room and saw a raised red welt bleeding upon her face where she had been slapped full force by an invisible hand. That night they left and stayed with Sir George Whitehouse, where they would regularly turn up at all hours of the night having been scared witless and desperate to escape any harm from the malign forces directed at Marianne. As the house groaned and the activity grew, windows would mysteriously shatter as the house began to speak its terrifying tale. Marianne was thrown from her bed across the room whilst she slept. The terror peaked one night when a mattress was held over her face causing her to fall unconscious. The house did not like Marianne. One night during Price's investigation the famous writing on the wall appeared in the hall close to the kitchen, somewhat more accepting of Marianne begging "Marianne, get help" and the words "light, Mass, Prayers" drawn in graphite roughly four feet off the ground. The writing was traced and photographed. With Reverend Foyster's health dramatically declining, the couple abandoned the parish in 1935 and due to the undesirable occurrences, no rector could be found to replace him. This led to the church permanently closing Borley Rectory and combining its parish with another, with duties shared between them.

With the rectory abandoned Price sprang into action and leased the grounds and to assist him in his investigations he collected a force of nearly fifty professionals, ranging from many false mediums to seekers of unusual pleasures.

Whilst conducting a séance in the library he met the entity named Marie Lairre whose story blended perfectly with that of the nun haunting the land and whilst begging for a Catholic burial became linked to the writing on the wall. At another meeting a spirit spoke, threatening to burn the house down and saying that human remains would be uncovered afterwards. Eleven months later, new owner Captain William Hart Gregson knocked over an oil lamp whilst organising the library. The fire spread and gutted the building. The insurance claim was made void by a suspicion that the fire was no accident.

Just before the outbreak of WWII an excavation began in the cellar where the remains of a young woman were found. Was this enough evidence to prove the hauntings to be real? The remains were given a respectful Christian burial at a nearby church hopefully allowing her sprit to finally be laid to rest.

6. SUTTON HOO

It's a Frigedæg in the year 520 AD

In the early hours of the morning the birds are singing for the sun. The river, named Deben by the locals, is almost still with a thick mist that swirls in the cool light breeze. The water parts as the prow of a wooden rowing ship glides towards the bullrushes lining the banks. After a time, the thickset travellers haul the boat from the water. Using boles of wood as rollers, the large group heave the vessel a hundred feet from the water to a trench some ten feet deep. Once in the sand the carpenters use wood sourced by the men to begin the task of constructing a chamber fit for a warrior, a king over all the land. The settlers stand by as the man, leader of the Wuffingas, is laid to rest. Sword in hand and his gleaming treasures by his side he begins the arduous journey from one life to the next. A huge mound reaching the sky is raised upon his final resting place. The time for festivities begins.

In 1926, Edith Pretty and her husband Frank, a retired colonel, bought the 526-acre Sutton Hoo estate near Woodbridge, Suffolk. In 1930 at the age of forty-seven Edith gave birth to their son Robert Dempsey Pretty, making the couple's life complete. Edith, fascinated by archaeology, was naturally curious about the various mounds dotting the fields nearby. In 1934, Frank died leaving Edith as a single mother. Devastated she retired from society, spending her lonely days studying archaeology and concentrating on her love of the occult. After a fellow spiritualist had a vision of ships and ancient warriors amongst the mounds her curiosity grew and in 1937, after a conversation with a friend, she followed their advice and contacted Guy Maynard, curator of the Ipswich Museum. He, after viewing the mysterious tumuli or mounds, invited self-taught archaeologist Basil Brown to view the site.

After agreeing to the terms Basil began the investigation alongside the estate's labourers using traditional archaeological methods and for lack of professional tools set about digging with a coal shovel and a pastry brush! Between 1937 and 1938 Basil and his hardworking team excavated three mounds with very few results. Digs in both Tudor times and during the 1860s had stripped the earth bare except for one tantalising find, a rusted rivet. This was very exciting as it indicated that the team could have a similar discovery to that nearby at Snape, a ship burial. After the second season Basil returned to his previous job for Ipswich Museum with a promise of a further season's work ahead.

At the beginning of May 1939, whilst excavating the mound selected by Mrs Pretty, Basil was growing despondent after finding evidence of treasure hunters once again but he then came to a realisation. He concluded that he was not digging in the centre as the mound had changed shape over the years. Adjusting his trenches, he began again using a different technique in the revised location. On 11th May 1939 an elated Basil cycled to Ipswich Museum with more rivets to show Mr Maynard. Maynard advised caution as, based on the knowledge of similar burials in Norway, the team were now expecting to find a ship burial under the shifting sands. Piece by piece a shadow appeared of a wooden rowing boat 27 metres long and of Saxon origin which confirmed Basil's first suspicions. On 6th June with the word spreading amongst the archaeological community, the excavation was now taken over by a team of professional archaeologists headed by Charles Phillips, a Fellow of Selwyn College, Cambridge, with Basil working alongside. Eight days later the team reached the centre of the construction and found the collapsed chamber with a complete set of chain mail, a jewel-encrusted sword and 263 items of gold and silver. It was then that they had to contact the police to guard the area from treasure hunters. The finds included shoulder clasps for a cloak, belt buckles, weapons and jewellery all made by highly skilled goldsmiths, proving the theory of the tumultuous and backward Dark Ages to be far from the truth. The priceless burial at Sutton Hoo was the greatest discovery of Basil's life. However, as the press descended and the coroner's inquest loomed, Basil was already being pushed aside with Ipswich Museum claiming the discovery.

Reported in the newspapers in August 1939, the inquiry began in the wooden army hut used as the town hall in Sutton. The field opposite held the vehicles of over two hundred people crammed into the hut. Before the coroner, rows of wooden boxes, nailed and sealed shut with wax were carefully opened, assisted by police, and gently placed into glass museum cases. The items yet to be cleaned shone bright as if brand new. Before a Jury of fifteen men five topics were up for discussion. The place of the find? Can the owner be found? Who was the finder? Was it a treasure trove? and finally, backed up by two typewritten sheets of what we now call A4 paper, a list of what was found. After twenty minutes' discussion the jury returned, declaring that the items were not to be classed as treasure and unless the crown intervened the priceless finds belonged to Mrs Pretty. At the time it was stated that Mrs Pretty was unsure what she was going to do with it all. Basil pulled out of the proceedings and ensured that the ship was carefully buried, topped with bracken to protect the whisper in the sand.

Mrs Pretty, with no request for payment, donated the entire haul to the British Museum. As the second world war was beginning, the newly acquired items were taken underground once more to the safety of Aldwych tube station in London. Unfortunately, all the drawings taken of the site were destroyed above ground by fire.

After the war Herbert Maryon, a conservator at the British Museum, brought the finds to the surface and whilst studying the assemblage found metal plates decorated with warriors and their weapons in full battle dress. Once reconstructed the famous helmet stared back at him surrounded by garnets from Sri Lanka. The helmet is now one of the most recognisable archaeological finds in history.

The Venerable Bede, writing a century later, named the buried king as King Raedwald who was the leader of the Wuffingas in East Anglia at the time, with authority over all the bretwaldas or over-kings. Historians have also made connections to the Beowulf poem where Scyld Scefing is described at his burial within a ship surrounded by grave goods.

Since the famous discovery several digs have taken place uncovering a second smaller ship and echoes of human remains called sand bodies that have left their shadows in the ground. These graves contained remains which were headless and bound by the feet and ankles. Mound 14 contained the only female burial within the mounds, suspected to be Raedwold's queen. Thirty-nine graves in the vicinity are suspected to be those of Christian people buried in un-consecrated ground. The graveyard, once of kings, became the final resting place of sinful Christians.

In 1991, Mound 17 revealed a male burial inside a tree trunk coffin with his weapons beside him. Close by in another grave was his horse. Whilst work was underway Mound 1 was fully reconstructed.

An Anglo-Saxon burial ground was also uncovered in 2000 whilst the visitor centre was being built. Thirteen burials from low to high status were found, all bearing everyday items such a combs and bowls for the women and spears among the men, indicating that they were part-time warriors.

With dramatic advances in technology, it is now possible to use radar to scan the mounds without any further damage caused by excavations.

7. THE NEWMARKET BOMBING

It's Tuesday, 18th February 1941 - 2.57 p.m.

A girl walks upright wrapped in a thick coat, a scarf tied closely to her neck. Alongside is her mother, casually swinging the wicker basket containing their purchases from the busy market place.

It's an overcast day. The sun is battling with the cloud, not quite winning, not quite losing. The girl proudly pushes out her pregnant belly encouraging the attention of her neighbours who are lining up their prams outside the post office, all containing little chubby babies wrapped in wool.

A rumbling sound announces yet another aircraft from the local base on its way out to war. Yet this time it's different. The sounds of machine-gun fire pierce the air as one by one the bombs fall.

The explosions deafen her, replaced by a high-pitched ringing in her head. The air is quickly filled with a thick brick dust and suddenly everything goes black. A heavy coat of rubble covers the girl as she screams for her mother.

The memories, years later and still raw, are all that survive, the event not printed, in a misguided effort to control the people's morale during the endless days of war.

In Newmarket on that fateful day, twenty-seven people lost their lives and more than two hundred were injured from the blasts. Ten bombs were dropped from a single Dornier 17Z bomber along the course of the High Street, beginning at the clock-tower end of town.

The sirens had warned of the incoming attack, yet they were so often sounded that many ignored another "false" alarm.

The uninjured ran to tend to the victims, their friends and neighbours buried under rubble or bleeding from shrapnel wounds.

The intended target was thought to be either a large gathering of high-level military personnel meeting at the memorial hall or the two air fields close to the town.

Meanwhile from Rowley Mile racecourse, an air base in the town, Sergeant Jack Richard "Benny" Goodman was taking off in his Wellington bomber. Once in sight of the Dornier bomber he instantly opened fire and took chase, forcing the enemy aircraft away from the town.

Benny was certain he had downed the bomber and the discovery of a crash site near Thetford seemed to confirm his claim.

This was the first documented occasion that a Wellington bomber was used as a fighter plane.

2021 marked the 80th anniversary of that fateful day but plans for a memorial exhibition were postponed until 2022, due to COVID. The Newmarket Local History Society plan to unveil a memorial to those previously unnamed individuals who became victims of the war at home.

CHAPTER SIX

Suffolk
Specials

1. PLAGUE IN NEEDHAM MARKET

It's 1662 and as described by Pepys "a great sickness" has descended onto Needham Market, believed to have been brought to Ipswich by large vessels known as Ipswich Cats.

Symptoms started with a red circular ring on the skin followed by fever and sneezing then death within hours.

People believed it was spread by the miasmic theory of disease. They carried posies of flowers or chewed herbs to ward off the sickness.

Plague victims were separated into sick houses at the bottom of Bridge Street and if lucky enough to survive Airing houses on high ground at Darmsden.

A chain was erected at Chainhouse in the east and Chainbridge in the west. Money soaked in vinegar was left in return for food and medicine.

Bedding was buried in the back gardens and fires lit to dispel corrupt air.

80% of people in Needham Market died and it's said that grass grew in the streets.

Bodies were collected in carts and wheeled to the plague pits at Chainbridge on the Stowmarket road and the Lion Inn fields up the hill. During an archaeological dig in August 2013 human remains were found on the hill.

The Plague marked the end of the wool trade Needham Market was so well known for.

By 1665 the town began its slow recovery.

The last epidemic of Plague was recorded in Suffolk in 1906-1918.

2. THE HADLEIGH GANG

It's Monday, 25th April 1735

A man weary from his labours puts down his dibber and stands, arching his back as he stretches. He walks through the kitchen garden to the wide sweeping drive to meet a messenger straddling a sweating horse. Once they have exchanged greetings, he hears news that enrages him. At once he strides towards the stables and prepares his mount.

Upon arrival in Semer he makes his way to a 'little house' where the Customs men have stripped his barn bare. Inside a large number of men huddled in groups turn to face our man, their leader. A meeting takes place and the outraged gang of smugglers agree to take action at dawn.

The moon shines bright as it begins its descent in the sky, revealing the large gathering of strong labouring men, each one armed with a brace of pistols and other well-used offensive weapons. The signal is given and they mount their horses and begin the short journey to Hadleigh. They arrive silently and approach the George Inn, standing in darkness and empty of its usual bawdy crowd. A dragoon guarding the gates slumps in his seat, oblivious to the twenty ruffians approaching, weapons in hand. Unlocking the gates, the men enter the inn where, laid out in the bar the anker casks of spirits, await, ready to be reclaimed by the gang.

The guards, snapping awake instantly, set about threatening the group as they load up their steeds. Bags are abandoned; a struggle breaks out where the drastically outnumbered dragoons bravely defend the haul. The crack of gunfire echoes off the houses lining the street. Our man, nose dripping with blood, reaches a calloused hand for his pistol, selects his target and fires at the guard advancing towards him. Surrendering, a soldier rushes toward his comrade, frantically trying to stop the flow of blood. With an ear-piercing scream an injured horse drops to the ground, desperately struggling to stand back up. Wounded men load up the remaining mounts. With the tea reclaimed the gang ride hard as our man leads his team leaving the town, quite certain that he is as good as dead.

John Harvey, the infamous smuggler and leader of the Hadleigh gang, was most likely born on 5th November 1686 in Hadleigh. He was baptised at St. Mary's church in the town. His father Thomas was a farmer. To become a leader of a smuggling gang Harvey would have to have been well-educated and literate enough to write letters, organize landings and have a good knowledge of maths to keep accounts and synchronize shipping movements.

A record of marriage dated 5th November 1722 shows a marriage to a Sarah Battle at Hadleigh. The couple had four sons and two daughters. Harvey must have done well for himself as he lived at Pond Hall on the outskirts of the town.

During the violent clash in 1735 Harvey shot a dragoon, one of three protecting the contraband. He died the next day. Out of the twenty members responsible for the attack, seventeen were recognised and arrested whilst John Wilson and John Briggs were sentenced to death and hanged. Harvey somehow managed to avoid prosecution for another twelve years!

It is reported that the Hadleigh gang had over one hundred members, each with two highly-trained horses. So well-trained, in fact, that if ambushed by Customs men with the simple command of 'whoa' they would bolt and when the smuggler returned exhausted the following morning the horse would be outside the house waiting! For the less well-off smuggler, horses were borrowed from local farmers though not altogether willingly, as tired horses during the day were not productive. However, if they refused, they would be intimidated. They were also forced to give up their barns as warehouses to hide the haul.

Gangs were highly organised criminals and would often join forces with other organisations in Norwich and Yarmouth, both in Norfolk, with up to three hundred members creeping out of their hiding places upon a cutter's arrival to bring the loads of tea and brandy ashore and quickly make it disappear into the countryside. With no coastguards at this time the shores were watched in a half-hearted manner. Customs men were both badly paid and completely outnumbered and could only stand and watch the crime go on, making notes on what they saw. Local police were often bribed and quite happy to receive goods to turn a blind eye. Interestingly there were many rectors involved in the smuggling business.

However, the commissioners had no trouble getting information regarding the transactions of the Hadleigh Gang.

On 11th June 1745, sixty horses were loaded with brandy and another fifty-three with tea, landed out of boat owner Thomas Cobby's cutter at Seizwell, Suffolk. Five days later eighty horses were loaded with tea landed from Cobby's cutter at Old Chapel. At the exact same time fifty-four horses carried off tea landed from another smuggling cutter, the Mayflower, with another twenty horses the following morning. The operations were so big and so frequent that in the second half of 1745, enough contraband was smuggled into Suffolk to be loaded onto 4,551 horses. This was made possible by a lack of revenue boats tendered for the Royal Navy because of the war in France.

In a typical smuggling operation, the leader would have identified several landing points. Organisation was key and timing vital. Once a location was chosen, an empty flintlock pistol would be fired to signal to the cutter where to land, despite any signalling to ships being illegal, and a spotsman with intimate knowledge of the coast even in the dark would guide the ship. Once in position the ship was unloaded into boats and taken to the shore where tea and brandy was packaged in oilskin bags and half-ankers. These barrels were made with a flattened side in order to transport them easily. A tubman would then carry the goods to the waiting horses and carts. Sometimes this would mean climbing a rope ladder up sheer cliffs whilst carrying the haul. Batsmen protected the tub carriers. They were little more than thugs, well-armed with clubs or guns. If approached by the Customs man they would stand back-to-back a yard apart forming a tunnel for the tubman to run through. Clashes were inevitable but the customs men, outnumbered, would have no option but to allow the organization to continue without any disturbance. With the penalty for smuggling being death the gang members were desperate and would do anything to escape. Once loaded the goods were spirited away, disappearing into isolated barns and ready dug spaces under the ground.

From 1746 the names of suspected smugglers were printed in the London Gazette giving them forty days to surrender themselves to the law. If they did not, they were declared felons by His Majesty's Privy Council and upon capture would suffer the consequences: death. The bodies were then to be hung from a gibbet around the coast. The £500 bounty on their heads made people much more likely to betray the gangs and there was also the offer of a free pardon for any smuggler who identified their fellow gang members.

By the time the law crept up on John Harvey an act had been introduced by parliament stating that any persons to the number of three or more, assembled with firearms in order to be aiding and assisting in the running and landing of uncustomed goods and goods liable to have duties paid on them, were liable for a conviction for that offence. They were to be found guilty of a felony and be transported for seven years. Harvey was shopped by two witnesses, John Tye and Robert Chenery, who gave evidence against him in a case held at the Old Bailey in Middlesex.

No smuggling story is complete without the mention of tunnels. If you question the locals in any town, they will tell tales of smuggling tunnels claiming their town had some. One such town was Harvey's home in Hadleigh. The tunnels are supposed to run from the site of a monastery at Lady Lane all the way to the church situated less than a mile away. These would be feats of incredible engineering. When challenged the locals would say that they had been bricked up in the past. Without any firm archaeological evidence proving the Hadleigh tale I am inclined to disagree with the claims for several reasons, one being that if they had been dug, they would have attracted attention and therefore not be very secret and would have been documented. Another thought is that the amount of excavated stone would have been enormous so where are the spoil heaps? Where did they dispose of the rock and mud? And finally, if they existed why has nobody ever found the entrances?

3. THE CAMPING LAND

It's Saturday, 1st May 1728

The excitement in Needham Market has been growing all week. The High Street has made ready with display windows boarded up to escape losing the precious glass set within the lead frames. The church has been decorated by the women and is green and bright, all ready for the festivities to begin.

The reverend, his preaching now over, watches the younger men with his face set in a frown. The town are itching to get out in the field they call the "Camping Land."

Once they arrive, the fit and healthy young men strip off their Sunday best and mark out the goals by driving wooden stakes into the ground.

The townsfolk line the field to clap and cheer for Needham and of course to hiss and boo the enemy, the men of nearby Stowmarket.

The teams are equally numbered with over a hundred members each, ready to do anything in their power to drive the pig's bladder home. Whilst music plays and children dance the game begins. It's a friendly sort of fight where both muscle and endurance of pain beyond common limits are on display.

The ancient East Anglian game of camp ball was first recorded as being played by the town men as early as the seventh century and is believed to have begun as a ritual Pagan ceremony with the ball representing the sun and the game ensuring a good harvest.

Played most often after the Sunday church service, this brutal yet thrilling pastime was at its most exciting when played on significant dates such as Shrove Tuesday or during May Day festivities. These words from an author unknown were often chanted during the match.

"When the pancakes are sated

Come to the ring and you'll be mated

There this ball will be upcast

May this game be better than the last"

A type of "Folk Football" or so called "Mob Football", it was the toughest and most dangerous game played with little structure or rules other than the prohibition of murder.

The game began with equal yet large amounts of players (thousands recorded in documentation). Its earliest form was played by opposing villages or even counties in the streets with the aim of the game being to put the ball into the opposing goals. Originally the goal was the village church porch or later the captain's own home.

The ball could be carried or kicked and often afforded the players an opportunity to settle disputes in so called manly tribal aggression. These occasions sometimes concluded with a losing team member being dumped into a ditch!! "Shinning" (a sharp kick in the shins) was extremely common and it was said no man returned home without black face and bloody nose.

The game caused so much trouble when played in the city of London that in 1363 King Edward III banned the practice with the threat of imprisonment. This law included all ball sports and local variations of hockey and was prohibited off and on until 1667. This however did not wipe out this almost ritual chaotic and wild pastime.

In a game in 1728 between Suffolk and Norfolk played out on Diss Common it is reported that Norfolk taunted the opposition by asking if Suffolk had bought their coffins along. The game was so violent that nine people were tragically killed. This event began calls for restrictions on the game and gradually led to what we now know as football.

Another interesting fact learnt in my research is the mention of a pightle, an enclosed piece of land, in this case triangular. The unusual name was documented by Sir John Cullum in his History of Hawstead as the "Camping Pightle". Being as close as they are and knowing the camping land to be just a slice of the original pitch size is this the origin of our Pightle off the High Street of Needham Market?

Up to 1830 the game was played on land specifically put aside for the sole purpose of camp ball and this is how Needham Market camping ground got and retained its name.

The Ipswich journal mentions our local camping ground as early as 1786. The camping land was up for rental in 1805 where two acres of land was advertised in the Suffolk Chronicle under the occupation of the Steward family who held the land for many years.

Luckily for the players of the game known as football these days, there are now many rules and regulations. However, I would like to see our handsomely paid players last just a few minutes in the game of our forefathers upon our beautifully protected Camping Land.

4. MARGARET CATCHPOLE

It's 1775

Thirteen-year-old Margaret Catchpole hurriedly mounts the awaiting Suffolk Punch and gallops hard to Ipswich in order to fetch the doctor for her sick mother.

Margaret was born in Nacton, Suffolk in 1762, to Elizabeth and Jonathan Catchpole.

From an early age she became a skilled horsewoman and spent her days working on the family farm. She had little education and worked as a servant for several families.

Eventually in 1786, she settled into a job, working for Elizabeth Cobbold at St Margaret's Green, Suffolk.

She became part of the family, even saving one child from drowning, and learnt to read and write.

In 1795 she left the Cobbolds and mysteriously became ill as well as unemployed. The only bright light in her life was William Laud who became her lover. William had become an infamous smuggler after being pressed into the Navy.

At this time Margaret met a man known by the name of Cook. For his own financial gain, he persuaded Margaret to steal a horse and ride to her lover in London.

It's Tuesday, 23rd May 1797

Margaret stole John Cobbold's roan coach gelding and within nine hours had covered the seventy miles to London and had met up with Laud.

There was a brief struggle as Laud attempted to put Margaret in a boat. Seeing this, a man named John Barry came to her rescue and a fight ensued where Laud shot Barry. He survived the injury and a price was put on Laud's head.

On the 27th May 1797 Margaret was arrested for horse-stealing and tried at Suffolk Summer Assizes, pleading guilty. She was convicted and sentenced to seven years transportation. In the meantime she was imprisoned at Newgate.

In the criminal records Margaret is described as having brown hair and grey eyes with a fair complexion.

After being removed from Newgate, Margaret spent three years imprisoned in Ipswich Gaol.

One night she stole a clothes line and scaled the 22ft wall, escaping into the night disguised as a sailor. She planned to meet Laud on the Suffolk Coast in order to settle in Holland.

She was quickly captured, arrested and tried.

It's 15th December 1801 and the Nile slips out of the dock, beginning its journey to the Australian colonies.

At this time Margaret wrote 'I am well beloved by all who know me' to her uncle.

On her arrival, Margaret became a servant and in time a midwife with her own little farm.

By 21st April 1814 she was pardoned but did not return to England.

Five years later, on 13th May 1819, Margaret died from influenza; she is buried in an unmarked grave at St Peter's Church, Richmond, New South Wales.

It was said that she never remarried.

5. MARIA MARTEN

It's Friday, 18th May 1827 and the red hot sun beats down upon a woman dressed in men's clothes, eagerly awaiting her lover in the cool shade.

That same day a suspicious-looking man glances behind him as he lumbers up Barnfield Hill heading towards the local landmark, the Red Barn.

Maria Marten was born on 24th July 1801 to Thomas and Grace Marten in Polstead, Suffolk. A quiet and intelligent child, she was sent to a clergyman's home in Layham where she helped in the nursery. Her mother died when she was nine leaving her to care for her siblings. Maria had a tendency to find wealthy young men attractive.

At seventeen she fell pregnant with Thomas Corder's child but the baby died. Her second child, Thomas Henry Matthews, was born after a fling with Peter Matthews who paid her a small regular allowance.

In 1826 she began an affair with William Corder, the younger brother of Thomas and she fell pregnant for the third time. The baby was very sickly and died of illness before a month old. Corder, apparently intending to marry Maria, kept making excuses and stalling the wedding.

On that Friday, 18th May 1827, Corder had arrived at Maria's cottage after hearing a rumour that she was about to be prosecuted for having bastard children. He suggested to Maria that she should dress in men's clothes to avoid the police and meet him in the Red Barn so that they could elope to Ipswich.

Maria Marten was never seen alive again.

William Corder was born on 21st June 1804 in Polstead, Suffolk.

He was known as Foxy at school for his sly manner. As a boy he feloniously sold his father's pigs and narrowly avoided a clash with the law. He forged a cheque for £93 and assisted local thief Samuel 'Beauty' Smith to steal a pig. As a result he was sent in shame to London, only coming back to Polstead when Thomas tragically drowned in a frozen pond. The father and three brothers all died within three months of each other and William was left to run the farm.

After that fateful meeting in the Red Barn, Corder fled but cunningly wrote letters to Maria's family, stating that they were living on the Isle of Wight, making excuses that she was ill and could not write herself.

Maria's stepmother became suspicious; plagued by nightmares she told police that Maria was dead, murdered and buried under the Red Barn.

Upon investigation a body was found buried in a sack with Corder's green handkerchief around its neck. An inquest was held at The Cock Inn, and the body was formally identified by Maria's sister Ann. Corder was tracked down and found in Brentford at a boarding house for ladies, or a school for girls, which he ran with his new wife Mary Moore. He was arrested and the house searched.

Two pistols were found hidden away.

Corder was taken back to Suffolk and on 7th August 1828, pleading not guilty, he was tried at the Shire Hall, Bury St Edmunds. Hotels were bursting and thousands eagerly followed the proceedings.

It was said that Marten had been stabbed in the eye socket, other wounds suggested that she had been shot.

Under oath and insisting on his innocence, Corder reported that he was by the barn when he heard a shot. Running inside he found Maria dead with one of his pistols by her side.

Inside thirty-five minutes the jury delivered a guilty verdict. William Alexander charged Corder with murder by feloniously and wilfully shooting Maria with a pistol.

"That you be taken back to the prison from whence you came, and that you be taken from thence, on Monday next, to a place of Execution, and that you there be hanged by the Neck until you are Dead; and that your body shall afterwards be dissected and anatomized; and may the Lord God Almighty, of his infinite goodness, have mercy on your soul!"

Corder was also charged with nine other offences including forgery and larceny for stealing money sent by Maria's child's father.

After three agonising days in prison Corder confessed to accidentally shooting Maria in the eye.

It's Monday, 11th August 1828

A man too weak to stand is being held up by two others. Unsteadily he climbs the steps. In front of a reported seven thousand spectators a rope is looped around his neck.

"I am guilty; my sentence is just; I deserve my fate; and, may God have mercy on my soul."

After half an hour Corder was cut down and the hangman, John Foxton, claimed his trousers and stockings.

The body was taken to Shire Hall where crowds filed by till six o'clock.

The following day a post mortem by students from Cambridge was held where galvanism experiments were practised on the body.

Moyse Hall Museum posesses one of a series of death masks.

Corder's skin was tanned and used to bind an account of the murder and his skeleton, reassembled, was used as a teaching aid at the Bury and Suffolk General Hospital in Bury St Edmunds, now the West Suffolk hospital.

His skull was obtained by Dr John Kilner for his collection of memorabilia but after a series of unfortunate events he, convinced that it was cursed, handed it to a friend named Hopkins. In time, believing Kilner's claims to be true, the two men paid for a Christian burial hoping to lift the said curse.

Many years later in 2004, at the request of his descendants his bones were cremated and held at a secret location.

The fascination with the event saw pieces from the hangman's rope sold for a guinea each as souvenirs.

Over 200,000 people visited the Red Barn and stripped it for souvenirs. Even splinters claimed to be from the wooden barn were sold as toothpicks. In 1842 the Red Barn burned down and with nothing left of it, even Maria's gravestone was chipped down to nothing.

6. THE CAUSEWAY

It's Monday, 11th July 1904

A man strolls slowly through the luxuriant hedges heavy with the blossoms of dog and field rose. Ahead of him long green stretches of hazel, willow and St John's Wort line the two-mile-long path.

The village of Barking has been worshipping at the site of St Mary's church since 951, although in Saxon times it was more likely to have been a wooden structure with a thatched roof. From 1350, a stone and flint building much like we see today was constructed, taking over two hundred years to build. Barking had both Darmsden and Needham Market within its parish boundaries, which is probably why St Mary's is so large.

The hamlet referred to as Nedeham in John Speed's map of 1610 became its own parish in 1901, explaining why Needham Market does not appear in the Doomsday Book. We find it mentioned with its current spelling in 1277, in a survey taken by the Bishop of Ely. At this time Needham Market had a Chapel of Ease, a small timber construction most probably built for the pilgrims to break and pray on their long journey to the shrine at Bury St Edmunds.

In 1458, during the Wars of the Roses, St John the Baptist was built in stone. The documents show that the work was financed by William Grey, the then Bishop of Ely.

St John the Baptist church, being surrounded by houses, didn't have its own graveyard so connecting the two villages was the 'Causeway' a variant of Corpse-way.

All the dead of Needham Market were taken on a bier to St Mary's Church, Barking. A bier is a flat wooden cart, sometimes with wheels, sometimes resembling a stretcher. The coffin would be placed carefully on the plank and covered with a shroud. It's said they were very unstable and unless the coffin was balanced just right, it tended to topple over. The path was gravelled around two hundred years ago by the tenants of Barking rectory as a gift to the local people. It's rumoured that the path has some connections to the dead in another way however. A man walking the path one morning in the 1980s passed a policeman at the first corner, giving him a nod as he walked by. He turned to take another look and the officer had disappeared. This man being a respectable inhabitant said the vision was solid and he only turned around as he realised the policeman was wearing Victorian costume. There have been other reports of children in blue and a lady in a full dress and always ahead, it never being possible to catch up with her.

The local paper rightly points out the fact that a police station used to be on the corner of The Causeway at the Town Hall and after researching the subject found two possible names for the ghost: Constable John Baker and Sergeant (later Inspector) Samuel Garnham Reeve.

The last burial involving a procession on the Causeway was in 1914. After 1906, a meeting held at the town hall granted Needham Market its own burial ground named St John the Baptist Cemetery. A lychgate was erected as a memorial to the sacrifice of those of the local community who fought in the war. It was unveiled on 17th April 1921 by Brigadier General Samuel Eyre Massey Lloyd.

7. NEEDHAM MARKET BOMBING

It's Monday, 19th October 1942

A young girl of eleven sits staring. She shivers as the crisp air floats through the white mesh covering the windows. The trees outside are losing leaves, floating and catching into miniature tornados as they dance in the breeze. She becomes aware and hearing her name barked out by the schoolmaster at the front the room, she apologises and turns her attention back to her work, but not for long. A roaring sound above drowns out the teacher's voice. A brief memory of an air-raid warning slams into her head as she and her classmates all dive under their wooden desks in fear. A deafening explosion, windows shattering, glass falling. The screech of metal twisting. A deadly silence. Her ears pop and the screams of terrified children fill the room.

Two bombs fell that day from a single German aircraft, but there was warning. At 8.35 a.m. the air raid sirens had sounded but that was the norm and very little attention was paid by anyone on that occasion. The first fell on the High Street at about 10.20 a.m. The location is obvious as the break in period cottages to modern houses is dramatic. Several houses were damaged but four in particular took the hardest hit.

Number 32, High Street was the home of Ernest George Nunn. Born in 1882 in Needham Market to Jacob, a blacksmith and Sarah, in 1908 he married his sweetheart, local girl Edith Ellen Finter. Ernest was badly injured and taken by ambulance to the East Suffolk Hospital in Ipswich where he later died of his wounds.

Ethel Elizabeth Holder lived at number 41. She was born in 1879 to Robert and Elizabeth Burman in Creeting Close, She was killed instantly at the scene.

At number 43 lived Isabella Ferguson. Wife of Thomas she survived the initial bombing but died later at East Suffolk Hospital. She is memorialized at Ipswich County Borough Cemetery.

The fourth victim, Louisa Ann Baker, lived at number 45. Born in Stanton, Suffolk in 1875, the daughter of Philip and Maria Baker, Louise later married Charles Hayward Baker and previously worked as a head teacher at the school she'd attended back in 1878. This was to mark the last daytime bombing by the enemy.

The four civilian fatalities are remembered on the War Memorial at St John the Baptist Cemetery at the top of Barrett's Lane, Needham Market.

The second bomb hit close by in the playground at Needham Market School. Luckily it hit the front where the offices were located and no children were too badly hurt. You could still see the groove in the ground where the bomb hit, even when I attended a long time ago!

An article in a local paper talks of the children from Barking being temporarily educated in the Tap Room at the Barking Fox public house with the smell of stale cigarette smoke and beer sticking to their clothes.

The memories of an aircraft crash on 17th October 1940 were still fresh in the locals' minds. A Vickers Wellington 408 on a training exercise crashed after flying too low and hitting power cables. The aircraft ended up on farm land, killing two on board.

Also, in 1942 a Junkers 88 was shot down, killing one of the crew who is now buried in Needham Market.

A little-known fact is that 1942 was not the first time Needham Market was hit by bombs. On 23rd September 1916 an L21 German airship, a Zeppelin, commanded by Oberleutant-Zur-See Kurt Frankenberg, was sighted close to Coddenham at 21.40h during WW1. He was apparently searching for Stowmarket. A High Explosive (HE) bomb fell onto fields and three minutes later an incendiary bomb fell over Needham Market, prompting locals on the ground to fire twenty-five rounds into the sky. Frankenberg responded by dropping thirty-four bombs over the area, including two HE at Badley Bridge. Sixteen HE and ten incendiary bombs landed at Creeting St Mary near Creeting Hall and Pound Road badly damaging farm buildings and killing six pigs. Further bombs hit fields at Brazier's Hall, then five HE and an incendiary struck Crown Hill at 22.43h in Stowupland.

ACKNOWLEDGMENTS

I wish to thank several persons without whose support and lovely encouraging comments Past Origins of East Anglia would not be here today.

So, Thank you to my lovely supportive friends both on and off Facebook. Also, a big thank-you to my father for the photographs and mum and Rob for their un-ending support.

To my husband Dave, my stunning kids and all those who allow me to spend every spare hour on my research and writing and are always there to listen to me talk constantly about the past, Thanks.

Also to Ellie Burkwood and Craig Smith my long-time best friends and both Admins and proof readers for my stories a huge thank-you if only you knew how much I appreciate you both.

An extra special mention goes to my editor (now friend) Delia Gleave who painstakingly corrected my spelling and grammar and went to the trouble of checking everything was just so. Without your help Delia this would have not have been possible. Thank you so much for being a part of team P/0.

I would also like to thank my Past Origins Facebook members especially these below whom without their kind donations I could have not published the tales giving long lost locals the last opportunity to tell it their way.

Tessa and the Aston family
Brian Bass
Richard Bevan
Ellie Burkwood
Mary Cadman
Wendy O'Dell Callaway
Gary Campion Flexible Digital - *hello@flexible.digital*
Laura and Dave Chapman also Madison and Cieran who are so loved.
Rachel Victoria Crooks
DGR Plasterers
John and Sylvia Drury
Michael Evans
Ian and Wendy Flagg
Paul James Oxford
Chole Anne Johnson and Ella Mae
Mary Phillips who always believed.
Sharon Rudd
Michael 'Bully' Shankland, 'A Burnt Ship' - *https://aburntship.blogspot.com/*
Ken Spink
Olivia and Lottie Springle
Springle Pubs t/a The Railway Inn - *info@therailwayfram.co.uk*
Irene Stubbs
Claire and Pete Suddaby AKA Grandma and Grandad
The Gale Family
To my loving family Ginge and Stanley Taylor xx
Joanne White

Sutton Hoo.

Pictures featured in this book
are courtesy of Barry Pullen.